I must also find joy in my friends — those who love me and support me. But it is a two-way street: I must also love + support them. This is something the entire presbyterate must do — love, support, show concern for one another.

A further reflection on making Jesus the center of my life: If the union with Jesus is to be deeply rooted, stable, then it must be nourished constantly by prayer. I am thinking not only of such things as the liturgy of the Hours, Eucharist and rosary, but the need of acknowledging the presence of Jesus in my life at all times, on a continual basis, and communicating with him informally and frequently. Friendship cannot be sustained without continual presence and communication.

M Y
B R O T H E R
J O S E P H

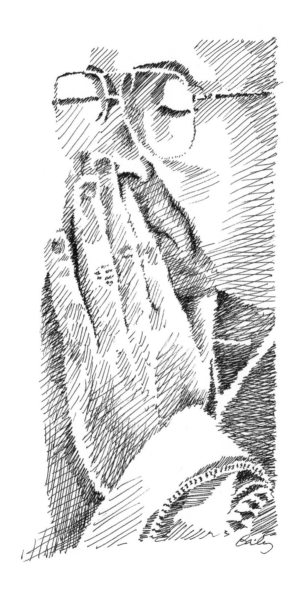

MY
BROTHER
JOSEPH

The Spirit of a Cardinal

and the Story of a Friendship

EUGENE KENNEDY

St. Martin's Press   New York

Design by Barbara M. Bachman

Line drawings by Ronald Bailey

Library of Congress Cataloging-in-Publication Data

Kennedy, Eugene C.

   My brother Joseph : the spirit of a cardinal and the story of a friendship /
Eugene Kennedy.

     p.   cm.

   ISBN 0-312-17118-8

    1. Bernardin, Joseph Louis, 1928–   .   2. Cardinals—United
States—Biography.   I. Title.
BX4705.B38125K47   1997
282' .092
[B]—DC21

                                               97-13306

                                                CIP

First Edition: November 1997

10 9 8 7 6 5 4 3 2 1

FOR KEN VELO,

SISTER LUCIA,

JOSEPH'S SISTER, ELAINE,

AND HER HUSBAND, JIM,

AND THE SMALL CIRCLE

OF TRUE FRIENDS

KNOWN TO JOSEPH

AND TO THEMSELVES

Acknowledgments

I WOULD LIKE TO THANK DIANE HIGGINS,
WHO SUGGESTED AND EDITED THIS BOOK
WITH A GRACEFUL PROFESSIONALISM THAT
JOSEPH CARDINAL BERNARDIN
WOULD HAVE LOVED.

MY WIFE, SALLY, APPEARS OFTEN IN
THIS NARRATIVE OF MY THIRTY-YEAR
FRIENDSHIP WITH CARDINAL BERNARDIN. SHE
IS A WONDERFUL CRITIC AS WELL AS AN
INCOMPARABLE COMPANION, AND JOSEPH
LOVED HER VERY MUCH.

I WOULD ALSO LIKE TO THANK
LOIS WALLACE, WHO HAS REPRESENTED ME
FOR A LONG TIME WITH UNDERSTANDING,
GOOD HUMOR, AND HIGH
PROFESSIONAL STANDARDS.

My
Brother
Joseph,

Chapter 1

THROUGH THE GIFT GOD IN HIS GOODNESS BESTOWED
ON ME BY THE EXERCISE OF HIS POWER, I BECAME A
MINISTER OF THE GOSPEL. TO ME . . . WAS GIVEN THE
GRACE TO PREACH . . . THE UNFATHOMABLE RICHES OF
CHRIST.

— EPHESIANS 3:7–8

Joseph Bernardin, the gentlest of men, was born in the harshest of times.

In 1930 South Carolina, one entered Eden after the fall, overgrown and untended. Few could recall it as a state of grace, spendthrift of its beauty and its bounty, exulting in the crops of cotton and tobacco that flourished from the saddle of the Blue Ridge Mountains to the flotilla of wooded islands that guarded its coast.

The Great Depression deepened a pervasive sense of loss and exile in the land. South Carolina dangled like the triangle of iron that once clanged to summon hungry workers to dinner. Now it hung silent, for the economy had hardly recovered from the Civil War when the stock market crashed in October 1929. Young couples discovered their destiny in that of Adam and Eve, forced to dwell east of Eden and to scratch out their living by the sweat of their brows.

Among these were Joseph (Bepi, as he was known) and Maria Bernardin, Italian immigrants with little English, whose son, Joseph, had turned two in April. A daughter, Elaine, would arrive two years later in the little house on Wayne Street in Columbia, South Carolina, that they shared with Bepi's brother Severino and his family. By the time Elaine was born, the cancer from which Bepi had seemed to be delivered by surgery returned, transforming the house of laughter and light into one of muffled sounds and drawn-down shades.

Life was as hard as the marble Bepi and his brothers mined from the nearby quarries. As Michelangelo freed figures from great blocks of stone, the Bernardins wrested happiness out of their harsh surroundings, contentment from their simple gifts, love deepened by the sacrifices it demanded, consolation and strength from religious faith tested by illness and poverty.

Joseph learned as he grew that hardship was not softened by escape—by backing away from its fierce energy as from a blaze—but by entering it as his father did the quarry, becoming one with it, whitened from head to foot by the dust-showering seam whose pulse he felt and whose heart he laid open daily, wrenching beauty before sunset out of the unforgiving rock.

This bred a deep, spiritual sense into Joseph Bernardin's bones, I understood after we became friends; you could feel it in him as you could feel his bones in an embrace in the weeks before he died. He grasped, as did the father he resembled so closely, that life was a contrary mystery as well as a grace, and that the latter was yielded only to those who were unafraid of the former.

I think of Joseph in profile against the abandoned fields and empty streets of Depression-time South Carolina, dutifully aware of the suffering that had to be borne if one were to become a man, the work of which was never done in a day, and aware, in the most heroic of human callings, that one had to scale the rock face with bleeding hands to bring forth from it the beauty of a saintly life.

Chapter 2

I DO NOT RUN THE RACE IN VAIN OR WORK TO
NO PURPOSE. EVEN IF MY LIFE IS TO BE POURED
OUT AS A LIBATION OVER THE SACRIFICIAL SERVICE
OF YOUR FAITH, I AM GLAD OF IT AND REJOICE
WITH ALL OF YOU.

— PHILIPPIANS 2:17–18

People often describe difficult passages, as Joseph Bernardin did that of his family after his father's death, as a time both hard and happy. His mother, Maria—deprived of education but not of wit, will, or earthy common sense— did not spend the five thousand dollars from Bepi's insurance policy, no small sum then, but banked it for the education of her children.

"Who will find a valiant woman?" This biblical question's answer, the image of a diligently weaving woman, foreshad- owed Maria bent over her sewing to support her children. Her skilled fingers grew hardened by the flying needle as she sought out every job she could find on the plucked-clean Depression plain. She labored for the government-funded Works Progress Administration, the WPA, whose blue eagle logo became a symbol for the Great Depression itself. Steady work arrived for Maria, as it did for the country in general, only with the Second World War and the nearby army camps' need for expert seamstresses to supply uniforms.

While Maria earned the food and made the clothes for her children, she enrolled Joseph in school a year early to give him a change from the house, whose fresh and easy joy was tainted by the smells of medicine and slow death. That boy—invested as fully then with duty as he would later be by the highest honors and obligations of the Church—could be seen clearly in the man I met a generation and more later. Meeting Joseph just short of forty, you met Joseph at five as well.

You could not shake hands with Joseph Bernardin without encountering his past and his parents in him, as the first sketches are in the final painting. Joseph Bernardin—called "the boy bishop" when he became one, at thirty-eight, and "America's senior cardinal" when he turned sixty-eight—was different, I thought, from most bishops and priests I had known; different, too, from most men I had known.

It was easy to see the good boy in him, already about his Father's business, indentured early to duty and the care of others, the bright boy who brought home the highest marks in grammar school and high school, the brown-eyed, black-haired boy whose gravity and determination to use all his talents were leavened by a forgiving good humor.

Joseph also cared for his little sister, Elaine, who, try as she might, could never provoke him into a fight with her. The sturdy little boy also learned to prepare meals in the house in which death had booked a room for itself. Rituals such as family meals kept the specter at bay, favoring for a few moments the living and their needs. So Joseph learned to cook, mastering the spaghetti alla carbonara that he would delight in preparing for friends even after he was a prince of the Church. And he learned the joy of sitting at table, celebrating the simple mystery of being together as a family.

He recalled his earliest days in almost the last of his days when he visited his cousins in Tonadico, the village made smaller by the white-vested Dolomites that rise above it, forming the massive stony seam of Italy's northern border. There his parents were born, and there, in the last year of his life, he joined his cousins in long, laughter-filled conversations after meals. These gladdened him and released memories of the first years of his life and the good times quarried out of the bad times more than half a century before in poverty-stricken Columbia, South Carolina.

I met Joseph Bernardin in 1967 when he was a young bishop and I a young priest. He was caring for another dying father, Archbishop Paul Hallinan of Atlanta. The latter, a gentle, scholarly prelate, had been bishop of Charleston, South Carolina, the diocese for which Joseph Bernardin had been ordained in 1952. Hallinan, who kept one desk in his study for official church business and another for his historical research, recognized Bernardin's unusual abilities, and after he became archbishop of Atlanta, he asked Rome to name Bernardin as his auxiliary bishop.

Bernardin served as vicar general of an archdiocese that

was growing apace with Atlanta, welcoming Catholics transferred to or attracted by the birth of the New South and its business opportunities. He mastered the secrets of administering an archdiocese as his father had those of the marble-filled mountains.

He learned more, however, than how to run a complex archdiocese from his mentor Hallinan, a World War II chaplain who entered fearlessly into the battle for civil rights led by the Reverend Martin Luther King Jr., who preached halfway across the city in the Ebenezer Baptist Church. It was Hallinan (Bernardin told me later) who showed him how a bishop could be a pastoral leader as well as an institutional executive. He urged Bernardin to take risks for the sake of what was right, and to spend more spiritual capital than he thought he possessed, in preaching the Gospel.

To understand what Joseph Bernardin was like as a young priest and bishop, one must understand what other priests and bishops of this period were like as well. The first time we met emerges from memory as a bright, excitement-filled day in that heady era immediately after the Second Vatican Council. Pope John XXIII's "aggiornamento," or updating, had loosed a tide of long-pent-up energy across Catholicism. America's bishops, learning to work collegially instead of independently, decided to fund a massive study of the American priesthood. That initiative brought a group of priest scholars together with a committee of bishops for one of the first planning meeting in the winter of 1967–68.

It was hardly an uninteresting group. Among its members were Monsignor John Tracy Ellis, the snowy-haired dean of American Catholic Church historians. Ellis had startled and spurred Catholics by a 1955 magazine essay, first appearing in the Jesuit publication *Thought*, and later quoted extensively in national secular magazines such as *Life*, asking why Catholics were not playing a greater role in the intellectual life of the nation; he chaired the history committee. Monsignor John J. Egan, famous social-action leader from Chicago, headed the pastoral section, and the bookish Monsignor William Baum of Kansas City, later to become a cardinal himself, chaired the ecumenical panel. Jesuit Bernard Cooke headed the theology inquiry at its inception, while Father Andrew Greeley oversaw the sociology panel. I coordinated the psychological research.

The atmosphere was steeped in enthusiasm. A systematic examination of the American priesthood was not only a first for the Church at large but one of the closest looks ever taken at a professional class of any kind. It promised insights across a range of disciplines to provide a foundation on which everything from priestly morale to seminary training could be improved. True understanding had to precede any real reform.

Yet the gathering was not without shadows or prophecy. Archbishop Hallinan had contracted a serious case of hepatitis and reluctantly withdrew from the session to rest for a few hours. Bishop Bernardin saw to his comfort and rejoined the gathering to listen carefully to the discussions. That afternoon I not only met this poised young bishop but observed his quiet yet intense style of concentration for the first time. In his voice and demeanor I encountered the tones and manners of a culture very different from that of—with the exception of the courtly Monsignor Ellis—the mostly Northern, big-city priests around the table. We all seemed in a hurry. You could hear the urban staccato in our taxi-hailing voices. He's the only one here, I thought, who is not in a hurry.

He was present—all of him—that day: the good boy free of guile, the top student taking careful notes, the dutiful priest and bishop ready to listen until the last person had voiced the last opinion, a well-tailored, white-cuffed gentleman who had not forgotten that his mother made the black suit he wore to the seminary. But you could also sense the deep foundations and steel frame inside him, this man so utterly serious but certainly not solemn.

Joseph Bernardin was again caring tenderly for a father half out of life and breath in a room upstairs. This reenacted his past and, although none of us could imagine it, foretold a scene near century's end in which Joseph would be the archbishop, dying as Hallinan did, remembering others with gifts, working to the last morning of his life, and cared for, as tenderly as he had ministered to Hallinan, by his chief aide, Monsignor Kenneth Velo.

Joseph Bernardin was in a way a peer of mine, born in the same year as Father Greeley and I. He would soon be leaving Atlanta to serve as the general secretary of the newly formed National Conference of Catholic Bishops. We were invested in his succeeding because we would be working closely with him as our liaison to the bishops in general. Still, he was the subject of the gossipy by-product of the often wickedly witty conversation that was a maintenance-and-survival mechanism for many priests. Joseph was talked of as a comer, one of the first bishops of the era of renewal ushered in by Vatican II. "You could go for the triple crown," one of the priest scholars observed merrily to him that afternoon. "First Washington, then the country, then the Vatican sweepstakes."

Joseph smiled gently, laughed, adjusted his large glasses, and moved back to the subject at hand. He did not use such wit to defend himself. It was the macho edge of clerical adjustment, the way men talked to one another in locker rooms, boardrooms, and barrooms all across America. But what constituted a real man? That perennial American question was answered better by personalities who did not have to prove themselves, such as Joseph, than by men who constantly struggled to do so.

Across the table, Joseph appeared pale, as if he never spent enough time out-of-doors on golf courses, in ballparks, or on fishing boats. He had earned this bureaucrat's pallor honestly, behind his desk, under fluorescent light, in candlelit church ceremonials. He seemed proper in every way, self-possessed and self-effacing; what kind of a man is he, I wondered, in comparison to the many priests and other American males for whom, like Ernest Hemingway, to be perceived as masculine was the first tenet of vigorous manhood?

In the next thirty years I would learn at close range, when nobody else was looking, how profoundly manly he was in a gentle, nonargumentative style that covered the tensile strength of his character. What struck me most on that afternoon was that, despite the clerical banter falling like fireworks all around us, he was knowing but not defensive. His lack of self-consciousness appeared to be one of the nonclerical fundamentals of his personality. For here we sat in a wood-panelled rectory parlor that reflected perfectly the men's club culture of the vaster priesthood from whose ranks we scholars had been drawn. There was no shortage of ego around the table.

The camaraderie that characterized American priests a generation past midcentury was on display in the good-natured masculine joking, the poke-the-shoulder fellowship that was not quite friendship, the vying for recognition, the listen-to-me, let-me-tell-you-all-about-this attitude that flourished in the clerical culture we were planning to examine—the Roman-collar-shielded enclave that made priests feel special, that gave them easy pardon for their failings as well as the automatic admiration of their people. Joseph Bernardin knew this world as well as any of us, and as a bishop, he was one of its first citizens. Yet he did not seem clerical to me, despite the episcopal ring that glinted like the silver pen with which he made notes that day. He seemed at ease with himself, at ease with us, at ease with the world.

A few months later, when I first visited him in his quarters, I was struck by how nonclerical they were in mood and furnishings. The bishops' rooms I had previously entered were often somber, decorated with reproductions of pious scenes and dominated by a picture of their mother, framed in gold. Some were so close to the sets for *Going My Way* that I expected to find Barry Fitzgerald dozing in the episcopal bed. But Joseph Bernardin's rooms were understated and tasteful, with original paintings, many on nonreligious subjects, such as the *Blue Desk,* as he called it, which hung later in his cardinal's study in Chicago—the rooms, in short, of a mature person on friendly terms with creation.

Perhaps nobody can track successfully how a friendship begins or why. My friendship with Joseph Bernardin began on that busy afternoon during which we sketched out our approaches to studying the priesthood. The world seemed young, a new age was beginning for American Catholicism, and we were right in the middle of it.

We became friends in a natural and unself-conscious way, not by trying strenuously to be friends but by recognizing that we were friends. Although I have come, of course, to regard it as an unearned blessing, it was as if, in the many exchanges of the afternoon, we shared a view of the flawed grandeur of men and women in general and of priests in particular. Almost everybody in the room was sympathetic toward sinners, but there was a quality of generosity of judgment about Joseph Bernardin—a central quality of his spirit—that allowed us, at day's end, to shake hands and know that we looked at things in the same way and that we could count on each other. In some mysterious way, we discovered that we seemed to have been friends even before the meeting began.

Chapter 3

I AM CONVINCED, MY BROTHERS, THAT YOU ARE

FILLED WITH GOODNESS, THAT YOU HAVE COMPLETE

KNOWLEDGE, AND THAT YOU ARE ABLE TO GIVE

ADVICE TO ONE ANOTHER.

— ROMANS 15:14

Traces may still be found, in cities like Chicago, of the classic Catholic family triad: one son on the police force, another in city hall, and one in the parish church. The host Protestant culture viewed the immigrant Catholic community as an easily identifiable lower-class group. Watch movies made in the Thirties or Forties to find Catholics portrayed chiefly as charwomen, policemen, and priests, almost invariably speaking with an Irish brogue. Of the lack of Irish American authors during that time, Jimmy Breslin once lamented, "They have the gift of words and all they write are parking tickets and insurance policies." He could have added "baptismal certificates."

Catholic education, a function of the institutional Church, would pay off after midcentury in opening Catholics to any professional opportunity in the country. But the institutional Church that had backed Catholic schools so strongly had little experience placing its most highly educated clergy in its own service. No organization supported education more than the Catholic Church, and none supported the intellectual life less.

From the great Catholic metropolitan areas through the middle of this century came a distinctive kind of priest—the classic American male, intelligent but not intellectual, central in any Catholic community—who was being affected, along with the rest of American Catholicism, by the long-overdue earthquake of Vatican II. Indeed, it was a priesthood just feeling the first tremors of disruptive transition that we priest scholars were about to examine.

Joseph's assignment as the agent of the American bishops for the intensive priest study was, as were many others he was given, almost a mission impossible: to be the practical manager of a major bishops-and-academics partnership. While a leading archbishop would always be the titular chairman of the project, Joseph oversaw the study that had been called for by Archbishop John Dearden of Detroit after he had become the founding president of the just-established National Conference of Catholic Bishops. Dearden, named a cardinal in 1969, became another father and mentor for Joseph, who on that long-ago afternoon when we met gave his administrator's dedicated ear to our discussions of the possible design of the study. Across the table, my distractable nature, the ever-scanning radar within, picked up and translated his signals—

his manner, his voice, his dress—into a scenario of his life and career.

You could feel the mannered South in him, the rustle of its long-furled flags in his voice, the journey he had made from the Depression streets, drowsy as Columbia's statehouse chambers, long behind him now. You could feel Italy as well, the stony earth warmed by a thousand generations of sun, its temperament as light and dark as its grapes, its worldly wisdom flowing out of a winepress fed by harvests of evil as well as good. Italian Americans who could be his cousins were coming of age across America: Mario Cuomo in big-time politics and Bart Giamatti in the Ivy League.

Most of all, you could feel his parents—his inner character as true as the marble whose secrets his father knew, and everything you needed to know about his mother in his telling us of her advice to him on the day he was consecrated a bishop: "Stand up straight and try not to look too pleased with yourself." There he sat, fully concentrated on a discussion of statistical analysis, everything he had inherited or experienced speaking to us clearly. He had come a long way to this table, to be fully and easily there, as both pastor and executive, his thirst never fully slaked for the work with people and with paper that stretched out before him, like the endless farm fields of the Carolinas, for a lifetime of harvesting.

As monitor of the priest study, Joseph quickly learned that priest scholars could be as temperamental and self-dramatizing in their displays as movie or rock stars. Once again, he had to remain a figure of credibility to both the bishops and the researchers. John Cardinal Krol of Philadelphia had been appointed titular chairman of the effort, and some of the priests immediately suspected that, because he was known as a shrewd and conservative churchman, he would automatically be a source of trouble.

As it turned out, Joseph would not be typecast, nor would he allow Cardinal Krol to be typecast. He developed a good working relationship with Krol, and such brushfires as did occur, usually over potential censorship, he quickly doused. Joseph met with both Andrew Greeley and me at O'Hare Field, for example, to review the conditions of academic freedom, which many of the scholars felt were imperiled. I can still see Joseph, seated in the small room in the American Airlines' Admirals Club, where we met, listening patiently, making notes with his silver pen, and acting as if he had all the time in the world instead of a plane to catch in an hour. He was patient and good humored and he knew that he had an understanding with me about working through such difficulties in a commonsense way. If I would try to keep the contributing priests patient by whatever device—humor, reassurance, or trusting Bernardin himself—he would see that their freedom was safeguarded. And so he did, never explaining how, but bringing guarantees that were, in fact, honored completely by the bishops.

It was a tribute to Joseph that relations between the bishops and the academic researchers were kept on a relatively smooth course. We all trusted and liked him. Unlike many other institutions or corporations, the conference of bishops never interfered in any way in the research or in the drafting of the final reports. Let no person think that this was easy. But it was natural work for Joseph—the labor he loved—to bring different groups together and reach an acceptable agreement without hurting anybody's feelings in the process.

Still, what a scene: Andrew Greeley, Joseph Bernardin, and I, born just a few months apart, in the midst of one of the most interesting projects that the American bishops would ever start, in one of the most exciting periods in American Catholic history. We would see a lot of one another during the three years before the reports were issued and in the generation and more of years after that.

Soon after this, in the flow of intense work that issued from that meeting, Joseph and I confirmed our friendship. It went beyond the gentlemanly cordiality or hearty comaraderie that marked most clerical relationships. We never played golf together, never went to a concert or the theater either. We got to know each other at work.

We developed, as men do laboring together—whether pulling a wagon out of the mud or drafting a delicate statement—a sure sense of which colleagues could be counted on, and for how much, when the weight came down on our shoulders. Soon, Joseph and I agreed on what he would later call "a practical way of doing things," and we knew that we could depend on each other—a conviction that, never spoken aloud or toasted with the clink of glasses at the end of a long day's work, quietly deepened in the thirty years that lay ahead.

When you end up like dockworkers shoulder to shoulder beneath the same heavy sacks, you learn each other's reflexes and timing, and how to move easily together. At close quarters, at hours odd and even, over a long period of time, nobody can fake what he is like. Joseph's spirit and his spiritual life were to be found in his serving the Church both as an institution and as a safe harbor in which to anchor religious mystery.

Some priests, indulging a temptation to cynicism, discounted Joseph's zeal for his Father's house as garden-variety ambition, marked by the concentration a man gives to climbing the rigging hand over hand to the top high above the hard planking of the deck. You either make it or—as with other clerics who miscalculated on their way up—suffer a long, fatal fall. Who has not seen such preoccupation with the self in the pursuit of some goal?

Although he was keenly aware of himself, Joseph never seemed preoccupied with himself. He was not, however, naive about himself. He knew which track he was on and that he was almost certain to reach an important destination in American Catholicism. His best preparation for that coincided with his own motivation. He was profoundly concerned with whether he was giving the full measure of his devotion and was dedicated to doing things as thoroughly as possible.

Nor did he ever appear to seek power for its own sake. He worked for the Church, always subtly, quietly, often under the worst conditions imaginable, bound to secrecy, and often without gratitude or appreciation, sometimes standing in the darkened wings as somebody else took the credit for what he had achieved. He would smile, shrug off the temptation to be critical. "You have to expect that," he would say, and turn to something else.

Joseph would carry out his duties in the dark, with nobody looking, exactly as he would have beneath the papal windows under the midday sun in St. Peter's Square. He loved the

Church as only churchmen—men of the church who do whatever it asks of them without complaint—can, in its every detail and demand, both as bureaucracy and mystery. His spirit and spirituality can be understood only as bound up with the public functioning and inner workings of the Catholic Church. Exorcising the devil from them, he encountered God in the details as a monk might find him in the desert.

A few days before he died, he telephoned from his sick-room to his chief of staff, Sister Mary Brian Costello, and asked if she had sent him everything to be reviewed. "I have nothing to look at," he told her, seeking out—indeed, needing to lift a taper to—one last candle of bureaucratic duty, the virtue that defined him at the end of his days as much as it did on the day we met.

Joseph had to establish what would later be acknowledged as his credibility in every venue in which he was asked to serve. "I have to let everybody at the table know that I haven't made up my mind beforehand, that I am not there to urge my view as the only one," he told me—then, with a self-mocking chuckle and a heartiness of tone that acknowledged the degree of difficulty he faced, he added, "And, believe me, it isn't always easy." As the mediator of the priesthood study, he was presumed by many older bishops to be sympathetic to the priest scholars. Some of the latter, in turn, treated him as if he were the bishops' executioner, ready to swing the axe of censorship at any moment. His style was to prepare himself for every meeting by reading everything, including the fine print and footnotes of documents that would spread a glaze on the eyes of men less well focused than he.

This anticipation of agenda items was bolstered by his

strong efforts—and these demanded old-fashioned acts of the will—to factor out his likes, dislikes, and prejudices so that the issues could be bracketed cleanly and objectively. This emptying himself of emotion and prejudice, instead of taking flight in distractions as many of us did during boring presentations, left room within him to grasp the conflicts that needed resolution. It was a constant theme of his life—the *kenōsis* (as it is termed theologically), or Jesus' "emptying himself, taking on the form of a slave," as Saint Paul described it. This was Joseph's way of purifying his work; it was the root and flower of his spiritual life as general secretary. He would deepen this foundation of his spiritual life, finding it sturdy enough to bear him through the enormous tests of his faith and character that lay waiting in the years ahead.

Yet we could joke with him about his evenhandedness, some priests reading deeper meanings into it. "You'll go right to the top from this job," one priest said in the banter of a coffee break. "Your record is completely clean. Nobody knows what you really think about any of this stuff." Joseph would join in the laughter and let us make what we would of his good-natured acceptance of the jibe. But this was also a sign of another prominent feature of his spirit and his spirituality. He understood how easily people's feelings could be hurt by even chance or well-meant remarks, and even though he accepted their inevitability, he went to great lengths to avoid being a party to this unfortunate side effect in any situation.

Perhaps most of us missed the spiritual core of his behavior in those days. It was, in a sense, rendered invisible by his lack of pretention, his obsessive style, which led him to go over matters almost too many times, his happy freedom from the pietistic behavior that other clerics mistook for spirituality. His inner life was, paradoxically, a life that inspirited his public functioning.

That many read ambition into his every gesture prevented them from seeing the purity of intention beneath the obsessive style, the unaffected goodness beneath his fine manners. (Do you think that it would be possible for you to finish this today? I'm sure that you didn't cause the delay. Perhaps we could start with item one again. Well, he's only human and we must expect many mistakes.) So gentle was his holiness that it was easy to miss or misunderstand it in that clamorous time.

Chapter 4

THIS IS THE CHRIST WE PROCLAIM. . . . FOR THIS I

WORK AND STRUGGLE, IMPELLED BY THAT ENERGY OF

HIS WHICH IS SO POWERFUL A FORCE WITHIN ME.

— COLOSSIANS 1:28–29

Joseph and I met just as the merry-go-round year of 1968 was about to start spinning, with events flying by so fast that not even Adam could have named them satisfactorily. I now see that during that period Joseph only *seemed* more akin to the priest scholars than to the bishops he represented. He was of our generation, all of us raised and ordained in the Latin Mass grandeur, regal glories, and hard-bitten discipline of an older church—"*The* Church," as comedian Lenny Bruce then observed, the only one that was capitalized even in the agnostic imagination. We had all come of age as World War II came to a close, at a moment of high triumph for the United States and for the Catholic Church within it, at least in the big, heavily Catholic cities strung across the top of the country.

But Joseph had no such memory, for he had grown up in one of the least Catholic places in the nation, deep in the Old South, where ecclesiastical records described whole counties as "priestless" and Klan crosses still burned like vigil lights of hatred against the night skies. Joseph's mother, Maria, received little of the acclaim mothers of prospective priests received elsewhere. Indeed, she had asked her son, who had just forsaken a scholarship for premedical studies, if he would be able to get it back if he left the seminary.

Joseph's skills as a mediator were honed on the sawtooth edge of hard times in an overwhelmingly Protestant culture. He was the weight-bearing arch in the structure of his extended family, the dependable intermediary between the home in which Italian was so naturally spoken and the city that remained on guard against any tongue that lacked the grace notes of the Old South. Immigrant Italian Catholics lived on a plain just above the lowest—a romanticized slavery kept blacks in their places as servants who might raise the children but must also ride to work in the back of the bus.

Joseph grew up knowing Catholicism as an island of saving grace in the broad alien stream of Civil War memories and manners. The institution of the Church was more a lighthouse than a powerhouse (as the chancery was termed in New York City). If mediation was his response of choice, his abilities and loyalty made him something like a first-round draft pick for a priest-hungry diocese—in short, just what the Charleston chancery wanted. And later on, at every stage of his career, just what the Church needed: a bishop so practiced in the art of reconciliation that it seemed as natural to him as breathing.

Joseph was quickly immersed in the world of the official, administrative church, learning to balance books and buy land as well as how to maintain pastoral care for the small population of South Carolina Catholics. So, although he blended with us big-city priest professors, his differences were at least as many as his similarities. He identified with the institution that by his every instinct and assignment he was committed to uphold. We priest scholars, on the other hand, as Andrew Greeley put it, lived on the "margins" of the Church, in its shadows rather than in its organizational core.

Young Bishop Bernardin's life and work—and, one must say, his delight—were inseparable, so that he seemed grafted by an invisible grace into the administration of the Church. The priest scholars, by their talents and training, were programmed to wriggle, Laocoönlike (but successfully to free themselves), from what to them seemed the python of such boring entanglement. Scholars live by distraction and curiosity, through long periods alone wrestling with the angel of creativity, so that they fill their freedom with demands as insistent as, but radically different from, those Joseph readily accepted. Give them reams of blank paper and they would find themselves filling them; give Joseph a hundred overflowing files and he would be himself in reading and putting order into them.

Chapter 5

LET US RUN WITH PATIENCE THE LIFE SET BEFORE US.

— HEBREWS 12:1

When Joseph Bernardin became the country's youngest bishop, its oldest were prelates of another time, first towering redwoods, survivors of many storms who wore their scars like battle medals. They towered shaggily over the fledgling National Conference of Catholic Bishops, an outgrowth of Vatican II's directive for collegiality, about whose inner workings they were ambivalent at best and disdainful at worst. They had risen in the age of hard-bitten Catholic growth and they had struggled to secure respect and rights for the Church.

If Joseph's great mentors, Paul Hallinan and John Dearden, were Irish American gentlemen of great polish and self-restraint, many of the other senior members of the American hierarchy were ready to hand their coats and hats to a bystander and take on, bare-knuckled if need be, whoever attacked the Church and its teachings, its pope or its people.

James Francis Cardinal McIntyre, a Wall Street businessman before entering the seminary, ruled Los Angeles at eighty-two years of age with what his priests called "an iron hand in an iron glove." He was unenthusiastic about the implications of Vatican II collegiality that called on him to collaborate with his brother bishops in the National Conference of Catholic Bishops.

Collegiality, although a restoration of ancient Church practice, seemed new and both unnecessary and slightly dangerous to the older bishops. After having twice turned the job down, the thirty-nine-year-old Bishop Bernardin became the first full-time general secretary for the Conference. Joseph's task was to direct a movie with this cast of veteran character actors and scene stealers, who did not like the script to begin with. Building a cooperative group of bishops—men who would cross their diocesan borders to work with one another on such projects as the priest study—would be as difficult then as orchestrating a cooperative European Union was to be a quarter of a century later.

As the son of immigrants, Joseph could understand how these Irish Church leaders felt. They remembered their parents' stories of signs that read "No Irish Need Apply" and of the Church's championing the cause of the unions against the robber-baron industrialists who tried to break them. They had joined the hierarchy when the rule was "The bishop is the boss in his own diocese, period." They were the sole authority and court of last resort, proconsuls in dioceses that had, in fact, been laid out on the model of the Roman Empire.

Still, the great trees had begun to fall. New York's Francis Cardinal Spellman had been found dead on December 9,

1967, not long before the priest-study meeting. He had died alone in his residence, just behind St. Patrick's Cathedral. Spellman had, because of his close friendship with Pope Pius XII, enjoyed enormous influence in the American Church until that pope died, in 1958.

His influence had been diluted by Pius's successor, Pope John XXIII, who had convened the council that had led to this new collegial mode of doing things. Quick to tears in his later years, the sentimental Spellman had enjoyed hearing his assistant bishops sing him Irish songs in the evening before he went to bed. Now Spellman was gone, although, in what joking clerics termed the "first soul transplant," he was granted the privilege of naming his successor, Bishop Terence Cooke, a sweet-tempered man who, as Spellman once told a friend, "was good with the money," and who was also ready to implement the decrees of Vatican II in the archdiocese of New York.

The tumultuous year 1968 signed in prophetically with conflict over the North Korean seizure of the USS *Pueblo* and the imprisonment of its crew. On April 4, Bernardin had seen President Lyndon Johnson sitting in the first pew in St. Patrick's Cathedral as Terence Cooke was installed as the archbishop of New York. That night, Martin Luther King Jr. was murdered as he stood on a motel balcony in Memphis. Riots broke out in many cities, and in Chicago a pall of smoke hung over the West Side, where burning and looting had taken place. Mayor Richard J. Daley, in some ways the civic counterpart to Cardinals O'Boyle and McIntyre, issued an order to the police to "shoot to kill" looters carrying Molotov cocktails.

On the last day of that month, Archbishop Hallinan died peacefully, and Lyndon Johnson, unable to find peace in the Vietnam War, became its casualty by announcing to the country that he would not seek another term of office. The country was woozy when Robert Kennedy was assassinated in a Los Angeles hotel kitchen after winning the Democratic presidential primary in California. As his funeral was conducted in St. Patrick's Cathedral, it was announced that James Earl Ray, thought to be King's slayer, had been arrested in London.

In July of 1968 the nation was at a roiling boil of unrest, torn by the war, the rise of a counterculture marked by drug use and free sex, planks in the political platform of the activists who were planning to challenge the old order and upset the Democratic National Convention at the end of August in Chicago. Nine days after Joseph settled in as general secretary of the bishops' conference, Pope Paul VI issued his famous encyclical *Humanae Vitae,* reaffirming the Church's teaching on birth control.

Two days later, on July 30, while Joseph created a collegial conference call that brought about a controlled-reaction statement from the conference of bishops, the Association of Washington Priests publicly supported the right of Catholics to disagree in conscience with the pope's teaching. Their leaders were named O'Donaghue and Corrigan. Bernardin's conciliatory approach held little interest for these Irishmen. Nor was the seventy-two-year-old Patrick Cardinal O'Boyle of Washington in a mood to parley on a matter that involved what he deemed the inviolable authority of the pope and of the institution of the Church. On the following Sunday, August 4, he had a letter read in all the churches of the archdiocese demanding total and unquestioning compliance by his priests with the papal teaching.

In that blistering summer, O'Boyle had set up a face-off with the Washington priests who dissented from the encyclical by citing another Catholic teaching—one about the primacy of conscience. He interrogated them one by one, cutting their number quickly from sixty to forty and, finally, to nineteen. Bishop Bernardin, deputed but given no credentials by the Vatican, worked behind the scenes to find a formula that would settle the situation in a way that enabled both O'Boyle and his priests to preserve their integrity. "I always try," Joseph said one day when all the pieces were almost in place, "to make it possible for both sides to agree without bringing shame to either. You want a win-win situation or you won't resolve an impasse like this at all."

By this he meant, as one of those involved later told me, that he would let O'Boyle or his dissenting priests present their side of the issue without interruption. When all fury was spent, he would calmly raise the question that was his signature overture for compromise: "May I ask if you have thought about the matter in this way?" That would be followed by a proposal for looking at the issue from a slightly different direction, from an angle that opened the matter to an inch of sunlight.

"Couldn't you priests affirm your loyalty to the archbishop and the pope in a forum that did not cause you to disavow your convictions about the supremacy of conscience of your parishioners?" Yes, they could, they would answer. "Then, could we begin, without violating that pledge, to dialogue without publicity on how to bring your viewpoints together? The wording would have to satisfy both you and the archbishop. But it would get us beyond this deadlock. Each party will give something, but neither party will lose anything in such a process."

He would then bring the same formula to the archbishop, who would agree to think it over and perhaps to accept it. Several times, as Joseph was about to put together an acceptable pattern of resolution, either the priests or Cardinal O'Boyle had second thoughts that scattered the all-but-completed design. Some of O'Boyle's hesitancy may have been inspired by Cardinal McIntyre, the octagenarian archbishop of Los Angeles famous as a take-no-prisoners advocate in dealing with his priests. He warned O'Boyle that unless he stuck to his guns, McIntyre would withhold Los Angeles's substantial annual donation to the Catholic University of America, of which O'Boyle was the chancellor.

Joseph found himself seeking peace in the midst of the kind of fight only the Irish can have, a brawl between brothers that ends with bloodied heads, no winners, and the unrelieved melancholy that Irish tenors sing of in ballads about young men lost at sea. We can see the conditions under which he would have to operate in this and other crises: his hands were tied behind his back.

O'Boyle, who viewed the issue as one of loyalty to the pope, was asked by Joseph, midway in his efforts to broker a settlement, "If the pope told you to deal with this in a different way, would you do that?" "Right away," O'Boyle answered, revealing not only his fidelity but the price he was paying in anguish for it. The question would never come to that, for the pope would not speak about the issue again and, in the ten years left to him of life, would not issue another encyclical.

Joseph could tell neither Cardinal O'Boyle nor the priests that Rome had given him his credentials. He had Vatican backing but not its visible support. He was, in short, asked to change the water into wine before this wedding broke up in a brawl. The wonder was that, depending only on himself and the trustworthiness honest people would find in him, he came as close as he did to settling the matter quietly.

The human toll of this protracted problem, like a hostage rescue gone wrong, seemed sad and senseless and, a generation later, without comfort or consolation. By the time Rome's Sacred Congregation for the Clergy accepted one of the resolutions that Bernardin had long before proposed, most of the dissenters had already left the priesthood, bequeathing to O'Boyle a Shakespearean king's victory, a triumph that cost the lives of some of his finest sons.

Joseph recalled this episode with regret for the rest of his life. "We were *this* close," he would say, pressing his thumb and forefinger all but together, "only to have it come apart." It was made sadder when he learned later that, for unfathomable reasons, none of the compromises he had forged and sent to Rome were transmitted to the Congregation for the Clergy. As Joseph observed, "We never had a chance—it was all over and nothing could be done."

Cardinal O'Boyle found no joy in finally prevailing. The banshee episode wailed low in his soul all his days. Who would not be touched at the sight of O'Boyle, on the fiftieth anniversary of his ordination, parting the lace curtains of the cathedral rectory with an old man's hand to see if any priests would arrive for the celebration, or how much Irish pride he sacrificed when he asked the priest who was to speak at the luncheon not to mention "the troubles"?

The memory of the exquisite suffering that was a by-product of that incident lived vividly in Joseph. He felt inside himself the hurts of the banished priests and of the isolated cardinal. He seemed to wince when recalling them in later years. It was, in Joseph's judgment, a mission whose failure was assured by the Vatican-imposed silence about his commission to carry it out. But it was a full initiation into the sometime ways of great institutions, the dark secrets of their self-protective procedures, which do not take into account, in their long calendar of history, the pain suffered on any particular day. Joseph would serve the Church but he would, if at all possible, use what Pope John XXIII termed "the medicine of mercy rather than that of severity" in settling future disputes.

Joseph also worked behind the scenes as an advocate for war protestors such as the Berrigan brothers, who were leaders in various movements to awaken the conscience of the country to what they saw as the evils of our engagement in Vietnam. Early in 1972, Father Philip Berrigan, Sister Elizabeth McAllister, and five others were brought to trial in federal court in Harrisburg, Pennsylvania, accused of plotting to blow up various ducts in Washington, D.C., and to kidnap National Security Adviser Henry Kissinger. The Nixon administration had assembled an all-Catholic prosecution team to send these romantic revolutionaries to jail.

I attended much of the trial of the Harrisburg Seven in order to write about it, and so it was a regular topic of conversation between Joseph and me. He, in fact, had written with Archbishop Hallinan a set of principles in opposition to the war years earlier. "You know, everybody knows," he said gently, "that these priests and nuns could never carry out these plans. These people are not criminals; they aren't really harmful. It is the war that is harmful." Indeed, the government managed to lose sympathy as its attorneys treated these pacifists, who refused to put up a case in their own defense, as people capable of overthrowing the government. The sentences were small in comparison to the large publicity the trial gained for the antiwar movement.

Joseph shook his head. The government had refused to budge; they had played hardball. At the time it was hard to imagine how these disparate elements—Joseph's behind-the-scenes mediation of the priest study, the priest protestors in Washington, and the surreal Harrisburg trial—would blend in the mystery of his own career. A decade later he would, as a cardinal, chair a bishops' committee researching and writing a pastoral letter on the morality of nuclear war. The priest study's intellectual demands, the Catholic peace ethic that motivated the Berrigans, the Catholic teaching about the primacy of the voice of conscience: Joseph brought the wisdom he had quarried from these mountains to a letter that would profoundly affect America's debate on nuclear warfare.

Chapter 6

LET US THEREFORE FOLLOW

AFTER THE THINGS THAT MAKE FOR PEACE.

— ROMANS 14:19

I handed back to Joseph the formal invitation from the White House. President Richard Nixon had asked him to join the Reverend Billy Graham and Rabbi Edgar Magnin for an ecumenical prayer service and preach-around in the East Room of the White House on the Sunday morning following his second inauguration, in January 1973.

We were standing in the marbled foyer of the archbishop's residence in Cincinnati, Ohio; a diocese Joseph had been named to head just before Thanksgiving 1972. The stone-faced mansion was tethered by a portico to the archdiocesan seminary, St. Mary of the West. It bore history in its every overstuffed couch and heavily draped window. Old times were also recalled by the paddle wheelers carrying tourists on the nearby Ohio River. The heavily Catholic city had been built along its cliffs and falls—Rhineland in the New World—largely by German immigrants over one hundred and fifty years before.

He tapped the creamy rich card stock of the invitation as if picking up the layers of meaning crafted into the looped ridges of its engraving. Here was Joseph in a characteristic pose, carefully examining the merchandise left by an eager salesperson. "You should put a sign on your head," I told him as he analyzed the invitation silently, intensely. " 'We Never Close.' "

He smiled. "You see what this is all about, don't you?" He turned to lead me to his rooms. The White House had not only sent him a bid but had also made a bet both artful and crass. This was a card from the Republican fortune-telling machine, giving its reading of Joseph's emerging influence in American Catholicism. I delivered this opinion as we doffed our Roman collars and settled into chairs in the Victorian study that as yet reflected none of the touches by which he humanized every place in which he worked and lived.

"Why didn't they invite John Krol? He's the president of the bishops' conference. He would be the logical pick for this." Joseph could not suppress the mild delight he took at being invited ahead of Krol or any other cardinal. He was not, however, seduced by the power that wafted off the vellum in his hand. He seemed entitled to these reactions, for they offered small consolation while identifying his dutiful obligations at the same time.

"Nixon," Joseph said, flipping the invitation open again, "wants to hold on to the Catholics who abandoned the Democrats in the last election to vote for him over George Mc-

Govern. He wants Catholics on his side when he starts dismantling the Democratic social programs that the Church has always supported." That was no lie. In the Twenties the theologically conservative American Catholic bishops proposed liberal social programs, supporting, among other things, the rights of unions and the need for a minimum wage. Many of these points, based on papal encyclicals, had been adopted by New Deal policy makers.

Joseph went to his desk in the adjoining study on the kind of intellectual reconnaissance I would witness times beyond counting, right up until a few days before his death a quarter of a century later. He wanted to find the documentation, quote the exact words he had written or spoken on some occasion, setting the record straight, taking pride in it, too, a surveyor displaying the carefully recorded measurements that kept a property line dispute from turning into a range war.

Joseph looked up, a sheaf of papers folding over his right hand. "Here," he said, his enthusiasm so finely tuned that it could barely be heard. "This is from my Christmas Midnight Mass sermon. Perhaps this is what got their attention. I thought about this a long time before I typed this into the final draft myself."

On December 18, 1972, President Nixon, after watching the movie *Patton* once again, ordered American B-52s to resume bombing targets in North Vietnam. Bernardin was preoccupied with this development as he vested for his official installation as archbishop of Cincinnati the next day. The unusually large turnout of over one hundred cardinals and other bishops for the occasion was another signal of how well he was thought of by his colleagues. Many of them were also distressed by the renewal of air strikes in the bird-of-prey war that still feasted on American blood and spirit.

Joseph had given his support to war protestors such as the Harrisburg Seven, but he would never join them in, or make his own, their dramatic tactics of civil disobedience. He would never raid draft boards as they did to splatter fake blood on the files. His way was that of reserve, of carefully researched and reviewed statements that were no less clear for their restrained formality. Such statements had staying power, Joseph understood; such documents outlived demonstrations and ultimately affected public policy.

He smoothed out the pages of his Midnight Mass sermon and read aloud: " 'In Vietnam, especially, we can only feel grief and dismay that the long and tortuous journey which seemed so close to peace has again been interrupted by violent force and massive bombing. It is not my intention at this time to assign blame for the turn of events. However, at this birthday of the Prince of Peace, I do issue a plea to the leaders of our nation and to all parties in the Vietnam conflict to halt the hostilities and to resume the negotiations quickly and in good faith so that this devastating conflict might be soon ended.' "

The simple paragraph had attracted nationwide attention. The White House could not have missed it, and that, in Joseph's opinion, was why he had been the designated Catholic representative to the makeshift service. "They want to co-opt me," he said, sensing the brass-knuckle, no-rules character of the public discourse into which he was being thrust as a new-generation leader in American Catholicism.

The Republicans knew, as Bernardin's brother bishops did, that he had received ninety-four votes on the first ballot to select a successor to Cardinal Dearden as conference president the year before. Krol had eventually won, but the vote was filled with prophecy about Joseph's future. If Las Vegas oddsmakers had raised their eyeshades in interest, they would have seen him as the overwhelming favorite to become conference president in 1974.

Joseph smiled. "And now I'm being invited to preach at the White House." He arched his eyebrows. "I'm certainly not going to insult the president under his own roof, but I will have *something* to say." He poured us each a drink, keeping to his theme. "They must have been surprised when John Krol backed me up with a statement condemning the bombing, too." He handed me a glass. "I will have to reflect a lot on this."

Ah, Joseph, I thought then, even as I think it now, here you are at the station for which Providence long before bought you a ticket; indeed, this is where you want to be, and you feel greater self-confidence now that you know the challenge of entering the lions' den of American public life.

He called me a few days later to describe the warm reception he had been given at the White House—guards snapping to attention, an escort to the sun-flooded family quarters to have coffee with President and Mrs. Nixon and his fellow speakers. After they descended to the East Room, crowded for this surrogate Sunday churchgoing that Nixon had introduced, Billy Graham spoke first.

"Billy," Joseph said in a tone that telegraphed his sense of having met his own expectations of himself, "spoke—and may I say that he speaks very well—without any notes."

"He winged it?"

"Yes, and so did Rabbi Magnin. They both praised the administration extravagantly, and Billy even called for teaching the Ten Commandments in school." Joseph allowed himself a mischievous grin. "The President seemed very pleased with that."

"Something tells me you were as well prepared as usual," I said. One Cincinnati priest said that Bernardin was so careful of his public utterances that, were he asked to offer grace before a banquet dinner, he would read it from a three-by-five file card.

Joseph paused to find a passage in his text. In his second inaugural, Nixon had emphasized themes long aged in the casks of Republican belief: rugged individualism, prosperity as the reward of virtue, his intention to chip away at what he considered the soft and costly humanitarian positions that had been emphasized by every Democratic President since Franklin D. Roosevelt.

"I gave a good general talk," Joseph said, "then I looked up and caught the President's eye as I reached what I considered a response to his inaugural emphasis on the rugged individual." Joseph began reading from his text: " 'The task is to eradicate that enervating individualism, based on selfish interests, that often works against the common good. That kind of individualism is illustrated in the demands for *absolute* rights for individuals without due concern for the rights of others, in the apathetic turning-off of politics because it is not immediately self-fulfilling, in a God-and-me theology that ignores the institution and the realities of social concern.' "

Joseph paused and told me that the room had grown quiet

as he read these pointed but hardly inflammatory words. Joseph picked up where he left off: " 'The philosophy of this extreme individualism is directly counter to the spirit of biblical religion, which emphasizes our relationship to others, our responsibility to neighbors, which is the expression of our response to God.' "

Joseph chuckled. "I worded it very carefully but there was no mistaking my meaning. And *I,*" he said, tasting that small morsel of delight that rewarded him for his preparation, "brought copies of my text. Neither of the other speakers had texts. So mine was the only one to go out on the wire services and was carried, I am told, all around the world.

"Nixon gave us each an autographed Bible. I think, however, that he may have heard the reporter who asked me what I thought of Billy Graham's suggestion to teach the Ten Commandments in school."

"And what did you say?" Joseph enjoyed a little prompting for a good line.

"I answered that I certainly respected the teaching of the Commandments but I thought that the Reverend Graham's proposal might run into some constitutional questions."

The President had been very cordial in that ill-coordinated manner in which sincerity gasped for air, but Joseph felt good about his mannered dissent from the hyperindividualism of the inaugural. The performance was, in fact, classic Joseph Bernardin: forget polemics, inject thoughtfulness and civility into a text, pay the price of being studied rather than dramatic, draw the circle carefully and firmly, let principle bind the discussion in the future. "I think it went fine," he said, exhausting his vocabulary of self-congratulation and turning toward his next project, of visiting the parishes and people throughout his new archdiocese.

Ah, Joseph, son and brother of understated duty, and yet more than that, far more than that for all of us with whom you became friends. We really did get to know you, everybody who worked with you. Work remained the chief mode of relationship with you—work, and illness at the end. As my wife said after your death, Joseph entered people's lives very gently, as if by osmosis, with no pressure, and suddenly we realized how much he had become a part of us.

Chapter 7

In October 1974, Joseph Bernardin was chosen president of the National Conference of Catholic Bishops. Two months earlier, Richard M. Nixon had wigwagged his way out of public sight as he climbed aboard the helicopter that lifted him away from the White House after resigning from the presidency. Word had just come that the former president had been hospitalized in critical condition with phlebitis. Not too long a walk from the downtown hotel in which the bishops were meeting, some of Nixon's closest aides, including one-time Attorney General John Mitchell, were on trial for their roles in the Watergate affair.

I attended that trial in the morning, listened to excerpts from the Nixon tapes, and, as if passing from murk to light, headed to the bishops' meeting to witness Joseph's election. I watched the only other Italian American prominent in the hierarchy, Francis Mugavero of Brooklyn, move swiftly to shake Joseph's hand before all others. The nation, I thought, might be suffering a crisis of authority, but the American bishops were not.

At a reception for the bishops that evening at the Apostolic Delegation, as the residence of the Vatican's representative to the United States was then known, John Cardinal Dearden smiled as a man might when watching his first son succeed him in the family business. "Now Joe can move," he said enthusiastically to me. He did not mean that Joseph could initiate theatrical reforms but that, partnered with a progressive apostolic delegate, Archbishop Jean Jadot, he was now in a position to implement the documents of Vatican Council II in the orderly, orthodox, structurally sound style that both men shared.

The principal thrust would be to enlarge collegiality, the restored mode through which bishops put aside authoritarianism, or decree from the top, and exercised their authority not in lofty solitude but in relationship to one another in a national conference. The same practical spirit was to be made operational throughout the Church, down to the parish level.

Joseph did "move" in Cardinal Dearden's sense, using his influence in the appointment of men solidly grounded in Vatican II theology to vacant dioceses, strengthening the National Conference of Catholic Bishops, and dealing every day with the problems—some of them having to do with stress fractures in the hull, others with the crew, and even more with the seasickness many passengers still suffered—on the shakedown cruise that was still under way almost a decade after the conclusion of Vatican II.

I saw Joseph from a slightly different angle than many of the priests and people in his archdiocese of Cincinnati. We spoke often on the telephone, and I saw him regularly at meetings or gatherings we both attended or in his own quarters in Cincinnati. He took me in on Valentine's Day 1975, after I had spent a long, frigid day traveling through snowstorms in a battered station wagon with the California grape-worker organizer Cesar Chavez, his son-in-law, another aide, and two large dogs. I was writing a story about Chavez and had accompanied him for days at rallies and had eaten only the fruit and pumpkin seeds the labor leader favored.

Joseph chuckled as he welcomed me, still trembling from the cold, and saw to it that I had food, drink, and a room for the night. He was interested in hearing about Chavez and of how, in a way different from yet like Joseph's, his personal life and his work were rendered inseparable by their spiritual fusion.

"What," he asked me as I thawed out, "did he say about priests?" Priests were much on Joseph's mind, as they would be throughout his career. What, he always wanted to know, could he do to help them? He would listen to anyone, especially somebody he respected, like Chavez, about how to strengthen priests in their pastoral work. That, as Joseph often said, was the frontline of the Church.

"He said," I answered, "that their communities like to have their own priest and that they see celibacy as an important part of their calling. Cesar thinks that if the celibate priest marries the community—and when that is done rightly—it is best for everybody. Celibacy makes them feel that the priest belongs to them."

Joseph, beset as president of the bishops' conference with literally hundreds of petitions from American priests to be free to marry, smiled appreciatively. "That's the best thing I've heard about celibacy in a long time."

The morale of priests was only one of the many critical issues that Joseph had to deal with not only as Cincinnati's archbishop and the bishops' conference president but also as a delegate to the international synods of bishops held regularly in Rome. He never complained about the work. He thrived on it, even though he did not lack anxiety about it.

He would move, soon after that cold night, out of the archiepiscopal residence into a three-room suite on the top floor of the diocesan offices in the heart of the city. I visited him there not many months later. The Wyethlike painting that he termed *Blue Desk* had been hung along with other pictures; statues and other objects had been tastefully displayed. He was at home here among these things that, in their intelligence, subtlety, fineness of taste, yes, and a tantalizing edge of mystery—what about these had spoken to him?—constituted an act of self-definition.

He talked of many things that night, sipping from a low-calorie can of root beer. He had begun the process of losing the extra weight that he had so easily added by eating the almost universally starchy meals of the rectory culture at that time. He had passed many tests but he was aware of those that lay not far off, especially for a conference of bishops that was just learning how to work collegially.

His greatest hopes lay with the maturing conference. The conference was the focus of what he did along with his labor in Cincinnati; that is what he liked to talk about after work in the evening. The bishops, he told me earnestly, come together as the representatives of local churches, and they should reflect the concerns of their people. "That is why they need to do a lot of consultation before they come to a general meeting—it isn't just a private club of bishops who issue edicts. That is the purpose of it all.

"We have a body of religious teaching that should affect policy. It is best to do that through the education of people who constitute the Church so that they, in turn, through the way they vote and influence their own communities, can do something about policy. That is the whole idea of the Vatican Council's statement on the Church and the modern world. We have to try to educate our people so that they are a leaven in society for the values we believe in."

He could not have fully foreseen that evening the crushing grip of the struggles that lay before him in building the bishops into a cohort of moral leaders working together. There would be enormous problems along the way. Joseph would later admit that the bishops' meetings with the presidential candidates in 1976 were close to a disaster. He had learned a lot about the media in the 1976 campaign, during which a few words spoken by him after he led a delegation to visit incumbent Gerald Ford would be distorted by the media into an endorsement of the Republican over the Democrat. Seeming not to endorse pro-choice Ford over Jimmy Carter while articulating orthodox Catholic teaching on abortion could not be sustained with the nuanced explanations that were second nature to Bernardin. During that Bicentennial Year he would learn a lot about how the media operated, which he would draw on in future difficulties.

Joseph would find himself, as Dearden had, choosing a course—support of the institution of the Church and loyalty to the pope—that was too strong for liberal reformers who wanted nothing less than revolution but not nearly strong enough for traditionalists who wanted nothing more than the restoration of the pre-conciliar Church. Steering an unmelodramatic structure-building course frustrated both groups. Bernardin was heavily criticized, especially by extreme-right-wing Catholics, who in their excesses went far beyond what most conservative Catholics thought or said. The irresponsible attacks by Catholic newspapers such as the *Wanderer* of St. Paul, Minnesota, would play a part many years later in traditionalists' going well beyond accusations of heresy and encouraging those who would charge him with sexually abusing a Cincinnati seminarian.

Nor could he foresee clearly how, despite all the obstacles, he would bring the bishops' conference to the point of issuing, in the 1980s, two pastoral letters—one on nuclear war and one on economic justice—that would attract national attention and lead to wide discussion and examination of conscience on these issues. As a cardinal archbishop in Chicago, his picture would appear on *Time*'s cover as the chairman of the committee that, despite opposition by the presidential administration, had drafted the letter on the morality of nuclear arms.

Chapter 8

. . . *NO VARIABLENESS,*

NEITHER SHADOW OF TURNING.

— JAMES 1:17

On November 1, 1976, I flew from Chicago to Cincinnati, rented a car, and drove to Joseph's office. Halfway through autumn the harvested fields had been smoothed over like bedcovers and the light on the Ohio River had grown angled and dull. The presidential election was a few days away, but many of the posters were already curled and tattered. Even the usually subdued buzz of archdiocesan headquarters was stilled— it was a holy day, All Saints' Day, a day off for all the staff.

Joseph was alone in cuff-linked shirtsleeves behind a desk, snowbound with paper. He smiled broadly as he welcomed me, ever the gentleman, ever the friend. "Sit there. Would you like a cup of coffee?" I shook my head. As he knew, neither of us drank coffee during the day. If I was restlessly anxious to talk, Joseph was quietly anxious about listening. I wished I did not have to tell him what he wished he did not have to hear.

"Joe, I have decided to leave the priesthood and get married."

"To Sally?" he asked gently, for he had known for many years the woman I had fallen in love with. Joseph had first met Sally, as he called her family-fashion, in the same mystery in which we all had met, the study of the priesthood sponsored by the bishops. Sally, professionally known as Sara Charles, M.D., had been a psychiatric consultant to the project. Joseph had, she remembered, given her a warm embrace when they first met.

"I know that you love each other very much. And I know that you will be happy together."

Joseph paused. His throat, much like mine, seemed dry, and in this intense moment, he removed his glasses and rubbed his eyes. "You know, when you called me"—he wiped his glasses with a handkerchief and replaced them—"and said that you wanted to come down, I was almost sure that it was for this reason."

"I was sure that you sensed it," I replied, "but you know that this isn't something impulsive."

"Yes, I know that. I understand that. And I know that this isn't easy. You're a very well known priest. This does not surprise me but it will surprise many priests."

"I've written up an account of everything connected with this. I've told things just as they happened."

Joseph reached for the yellow legal pad I handed to him and began to read it carefully. It was as true a description as I could manage about the history of my decision to leave the priesthood, which I still loved, for Sara, whom I loved even more. After several minutes, Joseph flipped the pages back into place.

"I'm glad you let me read this. I wouldn't change a word of it."

How gently, how generously and naturally he said this, I felt then and feel now as I recall it, for I know that my decision was disappointing for him, that it hurt him, that it was a loss. I would have understood if he had expressed his regret or even asked me to think it over. Some of my old priest friends re-acted later as if I had died, taking me off their Christmas card list and writing to my mother of the "tragedy" that had befallen me. But Joseph's affection did not alter. In the wordless moment that followed, his acceptance healed the separation that my action might have caused. His concern was for Sally and me and whatever he could do for us.

"I hope that you can write a letter of support," I said softly, "as president of the bishops' conference, for my formal petition for laicization."

He nodded. "Yes, I can do that. You know, I'm sure I've told you that the Holy See looks favorably on these petitions when the petitioner puts things in a certain way."

I nodded, for indeed I did know that if a priest said that he was suffering from a serious mental illness or that he had never wanted to be a priest in the first place, the department that processed such requests, the Congregation of the Doctrine for the Faith—the old Holy Office, of Inquisition fame—would endorse the petition right away. If a petitioner said anything else—such as the truth about falling in love, even though he had been happy as a priest—the petition would be routinely denied. Most priests I knew would not lie in order to get the decree of laicization. They rejected such a false presentation of themselves in what they rightly considered one of the most important and difficult decisions in their lives. They usually abandoned the process and got married anyway.

"Joe, I have not suffered a serious mental illness and I cannot possibly say that I never wanted to be a priest. Those things just aren't true."

Joseph hesitated a beat. "I was only thinking about how to expedite these papers in Rome."

"The Holy Office is granting these petitions," I said quietly, "so that they can build a file and point to it later on. They want to be able to say that the only men who left the priesthood were mental cases or never had a calling in the first place. You know that."

He pursed his lips; he wasn't agreeing, for that would lead him to damn a prominent congregation of the official Church. But he wasn't disagreeing either. "I must confess," he said with a sigh, "I've been so interested in helping men who have their minds made up get their permissions that I hadn't thought about it that way." He paused a few seconds. "And I know it wouldn't be right for you to present a false picture of your life. I know you. I know Sally . . ." He broke off, turned thoughtful in the deep quiet. Is anything quieter, I wondered, than a bureaucracy without the bureaucrats?

"I'll support you," he said forthrightly, "by attesting to the truth, as you have put it down in the account you wrote. I know it's the truth. The trouble is . . ." He paused again, for here, in this moment, in as secret a meeting as could be held, he would not violate our friendship, but neither would he violate his commitment to the Church in all the lofts and warrens of its administrative reality. I felt that what I was doing was sacred; he felt the same way about his obligations. He did not enjoy what he went on to say. "I cannot say that the congregation will be persuaded or that they will process this quickly. I think the way you want to put things may slow them down. But I will write a letter, telling them that you have been an exemplary priest, that we have been friends, that I know you well, and that I support your decision to seek permission to marry."

I thanked him but raised another question. I realized that I was letting our friendship bear a strain I did not want but could not help causing. "Suppose they put me off. They have done that to lots of men until they agreed to sign the protocol—'I'm sick and never wanted to be a priest.' I want to be married in the Church. If everybody thinks I've been a good priest, then I should be able to do that."

Joseph nodded. He knew that, frustrated by the congregation's procedures, many priests had married outside the Church or found priests who were willing to marry them without waiting for what was termed, in a quaintly medieval way, the "rescript of laicization." We had been friends too long for me not to ask him.

"There is a way around this, Joe."

We looked at each other across the breastworks of paper on his desk. We were brothers still, but I knew, as he did, that what I was about to propose would test any friendship. I could not expect him to say yes and it would be very painful for him to say no.

"*You* could marry us."

A new silence seemed to invade the old, to seal off the ticking clock and the distant traffic. Joseph was not dismissing what I said, but I had forced him into harm's way in that place where real friendship collided with sworn duty.

"If I did that," he said slowly, gently, "I'd be automatically excommunicated." He pressed his lips together, touched his glasses with his right hand. "I can't do that. Even if I wanted to, I can't do that. I understand and have never criticized men who have sought out priests to marry them even though they don't have Rome's permission. I understand that as a pastor. But as a bishop I can't approve of it officially or be a party to it." He paused again.

There was pain enough in the moment to warrant the utter quiet in which we sat together. We had walked a long way together but we had reached a fork, and was it he or I who had to take the one less traveled by, the one that made all the difference? It seemed that our destinations were now different. But not our friendship, never our friendship. Yet it was a mystery, one that he identified later to me as at the very center of his spiritual life—the mystery, found also in the life of Jesus, of letting go. He had to let go and I had to let go, too.

We talked for another hour about how to proceed. He thought that my leaving would cause a big reaction and draw a lot of publicity, especially in Chicago and in the Catholic culture throughout the country. I told him something that I had learned from a friend, Earl Bush, who was an adviser to Mayor Daley in Chicago: if you don't send out a press release, don't take phone calls, and don't talk to the press, there can't be any story. He shook his head in mild disagreement; this would cause a lot of talk, no matter what. Joseph later shook his head in mild amazement and amusement when I finally left the priesthood so quietly that occasionally I still get letters addressed to me as "Father."

But there were long months ahead, in which the Roman congregation turned me down with a single-sentence letter: "The request of the petitioner is denied." That happened twice, and by the next summer, Joseph agreed that I should visit the congregation in Rome in person. He arranged for a priest friend there, Bill Levada, now archbishop of San Francisco, to be my host and to guide me through the congregation itself. Joseph would send another letter of support.

And indeed, I visited the congregation in August 1977, and ascended in a protesting nineteenth-century elevator that was open to the weather of the inner courtyard to meet the highest officials of the onetime Holy Office. The archbishop in charge, a non-Roman named Seper, shook his head and told me that these matters should not even be handled by his congregation. He passed me on to another, more abrupt official, who seemed interested only in telling me, in derisive tones, referring to the letter from Joseph, "We do not care what Monsignor Bernardin thinks in this matter."

Finally, I was interviewed for several hours by Archbishop Jerome Hamer, a burly Dominican who carefully read the pages I had shown Joseph so many months before.

"Archbishop Bernardin has read this?"

I nodded, and he proceeded to ask me questions about every sentence I had written. The hours dragged by as he inquired into every imaginable thought, word, or action that might have been involved in my decision. He was not ungentlemanly, yet, by its nature, it was a shaming exercise. The archbishop was kind, but the objective was to humble the supplicant, to try to make him say things that were not true or that he did not believe. The protocol was shaming because it made room in its questions for lust but none for love. It was shaming because I was asked to write another statement but was denied the use of any of the typewriters in the congregation offices and got one only through the kindness of Bill Levada. But I insisted on recounting the truth of my human experience rather than accept a distortion of it.

Finally, Archbishop Hamer nodded to me, said that he would help process my papers, and told me to kneel for his blessing. He pressed his hands on my head. "Be a good Christian," he whispered and vanished with a sweep of his white habit into what I would learn was the even more complicated watchworks of this congregation.

Joseph only half laughed when I called him from Rome to tell him that they did not care what he thought about my case, that he had gotten a little side spray from the humiliation treatment. He seemed relieved, however, that I had talked to Archbishop Hamer, and expressed confidence that the petition would go through. We even managed to laugh a little, as people sometimes do when, after the river has taken the house downstream, that is the last best thing they can do before starting over again.

Neither of us could know as we hung up that night that a sense of humor would be essential to survive the years that would stretch out. A priest friend of Sally's and mine witnessed our marriage a few weeks after my return from Rome. But even with Joseph's intercession when he was a cardinal archbishop, many year passed before my official papers came through. John Cardinal Cody, the archbishop of Chicago when I first submitted my petition, derailed the process, claiming that I had been a well-known priest in Chicago and that my remaining there "caused a scandal to the faithful." He demanded that I resign my post as professor of psychology at Loyola University and move out of the city. Father Raymond Baumhart, S.J., the university president, stood by me, as did Joseph, for whom the delay in processing my petition was a small but real cross.

It had consequences, also small but no less painful for that, as, one Sunday afternoon after Joseph had been cardinal archbishop of Chicago for several years, he asked me to stop by at his residence. He came to the front door himself in shirtsleeves and escorted me up the elegant old staircase to his suite of rooms. We sat in his study. He gave off no shimmers of delight; this was business. He picked up a piece of paper advertising a large forthcoming gathering of Call to Action, a group of progressive Catholics thought too liberal by some bishops, at which I was to be the keynote speaker.

"This meeting," Joseph said, as if looking at an overdue bill, "is going to be held within the archdiocese. And you are a nonlaicized priest. You probably know that Rome has been after bishops who let ex-priests function if they are not laicized. Technically speaking, I am not permitted to let that happen either . . ."

Perhaps only close friends or married people can recognize the kind of pause in which we now looked quietly at each other. He did not want to say more. I didn't much want him to say more either. "Okay, Joe," I said, surprised by a twinge of the discomfort I had carried like arthritis in my bones ever since my visit to the Holy Office. "I'll just tell them that I can't make it. You don't have to say any more."

Joseph seemed relieved, for he knew that with all his influence (and that of another old friend of mine, John Cardinal O'Connor of New York) he had not been able to get my papers cleared. I was too eminent a figure in American Catholicism, some nameless official said, exaggerating my position beyond recognition for reasons that came out of an old and distant world. Our conversation carried enough humiliation for us both that Sunday afternoon. "I know," he said as we walked down the stairs together later, "that we are both practical men . . . " But we both felt diminished, as if by an old and wily sorcerer, when we said good-bye.

In May 1991, the Holy Office notified the superior general of Maryknoll, of which I had been a member, that my petition for laicization had been granted. I was in New York at the time and called Joseph to tell him the news, which he had not yet heard. I felt a kind of numb indifference, but he was overjoyed. He was freed, as I was, and immediately made plans to remarry Sally and me. That occurred in July, on a Sunday morning drenched in summer sweetness. One of Sally's sisters, Isabel, came from Notre Dame, where she was associate provost. Joseph's longtime secretary, Tanchie, attended, as did his housekeeper, Sister Lucia. He hosted a festive breakfast for us afterward. Seldom had I seen him as pleased as he was in saying that Mass, blessing our marriage, and celebrating our friendship at a meal. We were glad, too, but not nearly as happy as he to have fulfilled the request I had made of him, fifteen years before, to marry us.

Chapter 9

FOR YOU SUFFER FOOLS GLADLY,

SEEING YOU YOURSELVES ARE WISE.

— 2 CORINTHIANS 11:19

Joseph called me one Saturday afternoon early in August 1980. A few weeks before, a tornado had felled ninety-five trees around the house Sally and I owned in Michigan. A tornado more unstable and dangerous than ours had just pirouetted through Joseph's life as well.

Our storm went unnamed, but the one that grazed Cincinnati had been christened once as Carlton Sherwood, an investigative reporter for the Gannett newspapers. Sherwood had gotten through to Joseph by asking to speak to "Deep Purple," a conceit based on the Deep Throat from whom the *Washington Post*'s Woodward and Bernstein claimed they received inside information during the Watergate scandal.

"I took the call," Joseph said hesitantly, "because I've been accused of being the Deep Purple source to whom Andy dedicated his papal election book." Joseph was referring to Father Greeley's *The Making of the Popes,* published the year before. "*You* know, *I* know, and *Andy* knows that I'm not Deep Purple and that I had no inner knowledge of the conclave and couldn't provide any inside information to Andy or anyone else—that I wasn't even in Rome, that I was here in Cincinnati the whole time. Then Andy called me the other day. He was very upset because some of his notes had, he said, been stolen, and they contained mentions of me, sort of pipe dreams, Andy said, about me and Chicago. When Sherwood called, I thought there was some connection and decided to get to the bottom of this. Do you know Sherwood?"

No, I told Joseph, with no internal radar warning that this same reporter would arrive at our door in Chicago one late September afternoon, while my wife was at a medical meeting. He clutched an unopened bottle of Canadian Club against his chest, a crazed light flickering in his eyes. Let's drink, he said, until you tell me all you know about the Bernardin plot to overthrow Cody and the bishops' cover-up plan.

Carlton Sherwood, a burly thirty-something, had been on the Gannett team honored with a Pulitzer Prize for their 1979 exposé of some Pennsylvania monks who had engaged in low finance, selling off cemetery corners for gas stations, and other nimble but hardly inspiring behavior. When Joseph called, the Pulitzer Prize part was all I knew. What, I asked him, did you do?

"I drove down to his motel. I wore casual clothes. I wanted to find out where all this talk about my being Deep Purple came from." But Sherwood had thrown something else at Joseph, dear trusting Joseph, rendered more vulnerable by wearing a sport shirt, believing that a demonic reporter would accept his scout's oath that he didn't know a thing about it.

Joseph described Sherwood as having been "very aggressive" with him, claiming that he had proof that the archbishop had conspired to overthrow John Cardinal Cody of Chicago, succeed him and thereby gain access to the 1978 papal conclave. Once within, Bernardin was to act as the agent of an international group of Catholic journalists committed to rigging the votes to favor a liberal candidate and wiring the conclave to get the inside story for a later best-seller about it.

"Yeah, and movie rights, too," Sherwood concluded, warming to his task, sipping a drink. "First thing I want is Rome's secret file on Cody. Then I want a copy of the bishops' cover-up plan. How did you guys plan to pull this off? I've got the story." Sherwood had patted the breast pocket area of his jacket. "Right here. All I want from you are the details."

"I had never been through anything like that before," Joseph told me, no closer than I in intuition that this was merely a warm-up for wilder accusations in coming years. "He made me a little nervous."

A healthy reaction to paranoia, I replied. Then what happened?

"I decided to tell the truth. I told him that I didn't know what he was talking about, that I had never heard of a 'file' on Cody, that the bishops had no 'cover-up plan.' I told him that I was in Cincinnati during the conclave. Then he accused me of masterminding it all by phone and demanded my phone records."

Although Sherwood had made him very uneasy—Joseph reported that he had begun to perspire during the interview—

he had stuck to what he knew, the truth he drew upon in every crisis. I could envision these two men sitting beneath the throbbing air conditioner, the one polite and measured in every gesture of his soft hands, the other bullying the air with square, scarred fists.

Joseph's gentleness was fitted to an inner frame of remarkable strength and courage. He could draw on spiritual reserves of character deeper than even he knew, past the shale to his huge reserves of moral authority. That authority flowed not from his archiepiscopal vesture but from his soul and the sweet amalgam of faith and character that revealed how manly he was without being macho.

Still, Joseph was a first-class explainer. It went along with his obsessive goodness, his need to make the record clear and complete, to answer even the crank mail, to make sure that he was fully understood even by hecklers and those standing at the back of the hall. "I've written a statement"—Here it comes, I thought, and so it was—"to explain the facts in the matter. I'd like to know what you think of it." He really meant, I'd like you to say it's great.

And it was good, a detailed explanation of why he could not have been Deep Purple, pointing to his calendar to prove where he had been—in the office this day, confirming the next—a complicated account of a simple truth, almost always fatal. He knew some of the people but had never conspired with anybody about the archbishop or archbishopric of Chicago. What did I think?

It was like a manual translated from the Japanese about how to program your VCR; the truth was there in tortured terms and it would only invite more questions. But I could not give such a brutal appraisal to my gentle friend. A certain delicacy turned on automatically inside me in any conversation with Joseph, even in our easiest moments together. I violated this on occasion but in general found a finer self when face-to-face or on the phone with him. "Joe," I said in tones approximating his own, "perhaps we should ask whether this is something that you should explain at all."

I then handed on to Joseph the fundamental lessons in dealing with the media that I had learned from Earl Bush, who had been the Jewish intellectual in Richard J. Daley's inner circle. I had first met him while writing a biography of that mayor, and we had become good friends. I ran down Bush's rules for Joseph: Explaining keeps a story alive, because it adds something *new* to it, gives the reporter something to write about the next day. News is like a fire; it needs more oxygen to stay alive. That's what explanations are, oxygen. Deny the story oxygen and it will go out because the papers can't print the same story two days in a row.

Joseph was a quick and thoughtful study, even if such advice went counter to the ingrained habits of self-examination that made him seem as if he were taking his earthly finals every day and needed to post the results every evening. You never had to worry about even the possibility of Joseph's telling a lie. The problem was that he might tell too much truth.

"There's no need to issue any statement," I told him. "This Sherwood didn't have anything in his coat pocket. *He* doesn't have a story. He wants *you* to give him one. He can't print rumors. Gannett would never go with what he's got."

Joseph grasped the point intellectually but did not find it

easy. He worried that other reporters might ask him about the matter. "So you don't think I should say anything?"

"No," I answered, "and Bush's second law is that there is no moral obligation to return a reporter's telephone call."

Joseph agreed. Sherwood went off to Chicago, frustrated that his usual methods had failed him in dealing with Archbishop Bernardin. As Sherwood told me after his melodramatic arrival at our Chicago apartment with his ration of grog, "Goddam it, I couldn't get a thing out of him."

In his wild way, and before my wife returned to suggest that I turn him out into the late summer evening, Sherwood told me his theories. James Winters, a young editor of *Notre Dame* magazine working on a feature about Father Greeley, had come upon diaries in the latter's archives that outlined a plan, mentioning Bernardin, to rig and to wire the next papal conclave. Greeley claimed that these were imaginative musings, fantasies rather than facts, destined for one of his novels rather than for real-world geopolitics, and that they certainly did not refer to Bernardin.

Joseph, bred on restraint and self-control, mastered his longing to explain himself. He had kept silent two years before when rumors swept Chicago that the controversial and ailing Cody, living as lonely as a daughterless Lear in his North Side residence, would be forced to accept a coadjutor bishop with authority to run the archdiocese, and his name would be Joseph L. Bernardin. The papers for this change, destined for the next diplomatic pouch, were said to have been on Pope Paul VI's desk when he departed for Castelgandolfo, where he died (as did this speculation about Cody), on August 6, 1978.

The consistories that followed, electing Pope John Paul I, who died a month later, and, in October, Pope John Paul II, were supposedly the objects of the invasion and manipulation of which Joseph was scheduled to be the midwife. The alleged plot breathed air only when the *Notre Dame* editor came upon and copied Father Greeley's files two summers later.

Much was at stake for everyone in September 1980 as Father Greeley urged Winters to return the copies the young journalist had made of his diary entries. Sherwood had befriended Winters and read, in July, what became known as the "Greeley papers" and their supposed revelations of a conspiracy. On the basis of skimming them, he had called the Cincinnati archdiocese and asked to speak to Deep Purple. By the time he arrived in our apartment, the Chicago newspapers and other agencies were vigorously trying to buy or wheedle away the documents from the resistant Winters, who in the long run never released them to anybody.

But Sherwood had read and copied at least some and perhaps all of the pages and tapes. He was more than a halfhearted believer in the reality of the never-initiated conspiracy.

"Bernardin's your friend," he had said to me after his swaggering arrival at our home in Chicago, "and he was in on this right from the get-go." In the forty-five minutes or so he spent with me that day, Sherwood pressed his case: The diaries were dynamite. Had I known of the plot? Did I know the plotters? Then the request that revealed that he still didn't have a story: "Would you ask Bernardin to cooperate with me? I'll protect him as a source."

No to that and, no, I did not want to see a sample page of the diaries or have one or any of them under our roof.

Things quieted down after this flurry of activity. Joseph called back to talk of other things, including the presidential campaign and how the bishops' conference was maintaining strict neutrality. He had not heard from Sherwood again—had I?

Many times, I answered, and often in bizarre ways, such as his breaking into a phone call between my mother-in-law and me by telling AT&T that he had emergency, life-or-death information for me. Nothing of the kind, of course; just his idea of investigative reporting. (Who, my mother-in-law had asked after settling down, was that crazy man?)

Joseph laughed heartily, a let-go laugh, a good-riddance-to-Sherwood laugh. "Better he call you than me," Joseph said genially, thinking that this peculiar episode had come to an end.

At the meeting of the National Conference of Catholic Bishops in Washington that November, the month in which Ronald Reagan won the presidency promising to restore America's military might, the prelates voted to write two pastoral letters to the country. They would employ their collegial process to hold hearings and wide-ranging discussions that would involve as many people and experts as possible. One letter would be on the economy, to be chaired by Archbishop Rembert Weakland of Milwaukee. The other would be on the morality of nuclear war, and Joseph would be its chairman. "This," he told me after that meeting on the phone, "will be a test of how well the conference can function. It's our chance to speak as a moral force to the whole country on these matters."

Then he changed the subject. Had I heard any more from Sherwood?

Once, I replied. Sherwood told me that he had shifted his attention to the naval academy at Annapolis.

But nobody, alas, was to live happily ever after.

I learned shortly after this from Roy Larson, the highly respected religion writer for the *Chicago Sun-Times,* that his editors had teamed him with two investigative journalists, William Clements and Gene Mustain, to look into the life and possible scandals of John Cardinal Cody. There was a rumor that a federal probe had been authorized to find out if Cody had used tax-free money for nonecclesiastical purposes, such as buying a Florida home for a woman named Helen Wilson, who was not a blood relative although he introduced her as his cousin. They did not want to miss this story and they were going to start checking out Florida property records immediately.

Joseph, needless to say, was not happy when I called him. Cody might be autocratic, I suggested, but he was not a common thief. The idea was fantastic, and everybody had known Helen Wilson for years. Cody had been close to her whole family; she had been in Rome with him when he received his red hat. Despite his dismissals of the rumors, Joseph was glad to be alerted to the matter.

Joseph, however, was preoccupied with chairing the committee that was to write the bishops' letter on the morality of nuclear war. It was slow going, and the new administration, with Catholics in many key positions, was not eager about the bishops' potential interference in their restoration of American military superiority. Some of the bishops had, in fact, felt pressure from Catholic figures in the government and the military. (This isn't your field. National security may be at stake. It would be better if you minded your own business.) But Joseph was determined to see this project through. He had thought about the subject for years and was willing to pursue the bishops' education about military matters in view of attaining a well-informed pastoral letter.

Working on it with committee members as diverse as former U.S. Navy chief of chaplains Bishop John O'Connor and the antiwar activist Bishop Thomas Gumbleton demanded a diamond cutter's attention and sure sense of when to strike the blow that would yield the finest of stones. The letter—its composition, but more important, its delicate issues—became a focus of his prayer life. A few years before, he had experienced what he would still call just days before his death "a turning point in my life."

At a dinner with him, a group of young Cincinnati priests had challenged him about the amount of his administrative work and travel and his need to spiritualize his work even more and deepen his own personal life. At that time he decided to give the first hour of the day to prayer no matter what his schedule was. He kept that vow into the last autumn of a life whose already intense spirituality necessarily centered on his daily work. Heading to the airport for an early plane, my driver often turned up State Street toward Lincoln Park. There in the darkened neighborhood on the second floor of the last house on the right, the lights would be on in Cardinal Bernardin's rooms, where he would be praying before the city's day, or his own, began.

Fate's wheel creaked beneath these events as John Cardinal

Cody, whose once robust face had been ravaged and hollowed by congestive heart failure, consulted the office of Representative Dan Rostenkowski on whether a federal investigation of his funds was under way and, if so, how to handle it. Rostenkowski in turn called Earl Bush in Chicago for his counsel in the matter so that he could advise Cody. Get the truth out, Earl advised—the whole truth—as soon as possible, and don't tell any lies; lies come back to kill you. Cody was advised at the time by his lawyer Don Rueben, who represented the *Chicago Tribune* as well, and took pride in his reputation as a fixer—it proved that he had Chicago karma. Cardinal Cody, with more than a soupçon of justification, thought that a probe of his finances was outrageous. He decided to stonewall, to hold out against government inquiries as he had those of the *Chicago Sun-Times.* So what if he had separate bank accounts? Didn't he use one to help alcoholic priests and the other to finance the Church behind the then-still-unparted Iron Curtain?

What neither Cody nor, for that matter, Bernardin knew, was that Earl Bush and I ate lunch every week at the old Blackhawk in the Loop. There, midst the clattering china and the well-fed groups around us, we exchanged information on what was going on behind the rumors and occasional news stories about the beleaguered cardinal, and as matters developed, discussed how Bernardin could best be kept out of and away from this volatile situation.

The explosion took place almost a year later—a long, festering year during which the criticism of Cody was led by a relatively small group, Concerned Catholics of Chicago, organized in late 1981 after Cody, following advice from Rostenkowski, refused to comply with a subpoena from a federal grand jury and failed to make a promised response to the allegations against him. Rome knew about the situation but was proceeding slowly. Cody had many friends there, and his argument about the unconstitutionality of the procedures against him did not seem ill founded or ill made.

For Joseph, the summer of 1981 was worrisome. Every few days, somebody or some news organization called his communications officer, Dan Kane, with questions about the criticism of Cody: was it a plot, and what role did Bernardin play in it? Joseph prayed on the matter while at a meeting with the conference of bishops in Minnesota that summer. He called me from there, his tone down and reflective of his searching spiritual self-examination. The idea of becoming archbishop of Chicago did appeal to him. He recognized that human feeling in himself and admitted that he was frustrated at being implicated, against his every instinct and action, in any plots of any kind.

"I feel certain that after all this, I won't be appointed to Chicago," he said matter-of-factly. "I've been dragged into the middle of all this without having anything to do with it. I'm not sure what God's plan is, but I think that Chicago will go to someone else, and I will just have to accept that." This was Joseph speaking in the safe intimacy of our friendship, saying to me what he could not say to his colleagues. I thought of him sitting in some room at St. John's Abbey with a view of the wheat fields rolling like high tide in the summer wind, and of his life of duty and service. Something of his utter goodness and guilelessness struck me powerfully. "Joe," I replied, passing on a tip that Sally, my psychiatrist wife, had given me about him, "you're just a good Catholic obsessive putting your defenses in order. You're getting like the Irish, buying funeral bunting when they're perfectly healthy."

Joseph laughed, lightened his tone. "Well, maybe Sally is right. I feel God has got me in this for some purpose, but I can't think what it is."

If Joseph heard the cauldron gurgling through the summer, it tipped over on September 10, 1981, when the *Chicago Sun-Times* ran a front-page story, copied across the country, with a color photograph of Cody, stating that he had been issued a federal subpoena concerning his financial affairs. They tied to this everything they had found in their months of looking into the cardinal's life: his friendship with what the Irish call a "shirttail cousin," Helen Wilson; his long involvement with her family; his giving insurance accounts to her son; his financing and visiting, always with another priest, of her home in Boca Raton, Florida. It was more sizzle than steak since it provided no proof of anything wrong and, for many people in the know, not much of anything new. But the story caused a sensation for the public in general and a flurry of media inquiry. Joseph reviewed most of what was going on with me, and I, invoking Earl Bush's principles, advised him not to return any calls, not to repeat the charges, and to draw on his stores of patience to spiritualize this trying and mysterious episode.

Things got worse during the first week of autumn. Reporters from around the country had gathered in advance to see if anything further developed. During that week, Rob Worden, publisher of the *Chicago Lawyer,* began calling friends to tell them that he was procuring, in sections, the famous

Greeley papers. He told callers, including me, that Archbishop Bernardin "was apparently deeply involved in it." Everybody was welcome to come by and read a swatch or two of them. How Worden had managed to get the papers was never explained fully. James Winters, the *Notre Dame* editor, theorized later that Sherwood had read them over the phone to Worden, who had copied them down. This would account for their gradual arrival and for the textual divergences from the originals.

A dizzying paranoia sat on the city, a tingling cloud drifting in the streets, building up day by day, drawing reporters like pilgrims to some suicidal shrine. On Saturday the *Tribune* began distributing its Sunday editions featuring pictures of Archbishop Bernardin and Father Greeley and reprinting the thousands of words of conclave plans that Father Greeley again said were "fantasies," the things novelists write down in their notebooks, rather than a plan of action. Here, like diamonds arrayed on velvet, were all the plans to get Joseph into Chicago, after getting Cody out, in time for Joseph to be made a cardinal and to enter the next conclave to rig it as well as to steal materials: "He [Bernardin] has to be the one to do it. . . . It's a very sticky business, though."

"I just talked to Cardinal Cody," Joseph told me in a subdued voice that Saturday evening, "and I said, 'John, you know that I had nothing to do with all this.' He agreed, but there is not much either of us can do right now. If they think that they can get John Cody out easily, however, they are mistaken. He digs in; he's a fighter." What Bernardin did not know at the time was that behind Cody's reassurances was a determination to dump the problem at Joseph's door, if at all possible. He ordered his diocesan newspaper editor to send copies of the revelations to every Catholic paper in Ohio.

It was a weekend filled with rue and the explainer in Joseph began to demand equal time. He felt that the circumstances had become extreme. His name had been attached, on dispatches now being broadcast around the world, to the most bizarre behavior that he could think of. I could understand how weary he was of not defending himself even as I reminded him that his self-restraint was one of his most valuable characteristics and that restraint could kill a fiery story quickly by denying it oxygen. It was with Earl Bush's help that I wrote the sentence that Joseph agreed to issue as a statement Saturday evening and to repeat when he was queried on Sunday by reporters: "Father Greeley has said that these are fantasies, and that is what they are."

Joseph agreed reluctantly, uneasily, to this wording, letting go of the reasonable man within—indeed, letting go of ambition, of honest and deserved possibilities, letting go in faith, relying on the truth, if it could ever manifest itself, to make him free. First of all, I said, we have to control the possibilities of further obscuring the truth.

"Okay," Joseph said, "we'll see."

For the only time in our relationship, I resorted to vulgarity to emphasize the need to stick to the script. "If you fuck this up," I said after a long discussion, "it will be your own fault."

The next day, he was scheduled for a Mass in Dayton. Outside the church, reporters and photographers shouted questions at him. "Father Greeley," he said, as he had in a statement issued the night before, "has said that these are fantasies, and that is what they are."

These words were carried in the wire stories, the Sunday papers, and on television news shows. By Monday, Joseph, by not repeating the charges or adding anything new to them, had dropped out of the media coverage. The focus returned to Cardinal Cody and Father Greeley.

Joseph plunged back into his work without a glance to the side or to the back. He resisted responding to the prodding of the other principal figures. Sherwood talked often to me, asking me to intercede with Bernardin so that he could verify the so-called file or dossier on Cody. Cody continued to live in his own world, celebrating his fiftieth anniversary of ordination on December 8, 1981, at the Mundelein seminary rather than downtown, where he feared that it might be disrupted. He did mount the pulpit at Holy Name Cathedral for Midnight Mass on Christmas, saying to Father Timothy Lyne, the church's rector, "This is my last hurrah." He died, alone save for a hired nurse, in his residence the next April.

Joseph, ready to accept the end of his career, spent a whole day on October 1, 1981, with the apostolic delegate, Archbishop Pio Laghi, reviewing the matter, intermittently overtaken by his obsessive needs but keeping firm control of himself. It was, however, as he told me, "no fun, and quite shaky at certain moments." On October 10, he called me from Rome to tell me that everything had settled down and that things should be fine if nobody added any fuel to the fire. Later he told me that one of the things that they admired in Washington and Rome was how he had held the story to a minimum through his controlled way of dealing with the press. We both had a good laugh before we hung up that evening. I immediately thought, however, that it was easy to give advice but far harder to carry it out in the spotlight. It was, I concluded, Joseph's goodness, so transparent, that made him credible to the media and his superiors in the Church. His goodness was a secret weapon, the more effective because it was so seldom seen in public figures.

Father Greeley made millions out of his coincidentally published novel, *The Cardinal Sins.* I was asked to write an article about the Chicago tragicomedy for *The New York Times Magazine* but declined. Carlton Sherwood took an empty briefcase to the office of the editor of that magazine, tapped it, and claimed that it contained all the evidence about the Cody plot. He was commissioned on the spot to write it up. But he never made more than a beginning on that article, and by the next March, the assignment was killed. Nor did Sherwood deliver the book for which he had boasted that he had received a substantial advance.

On July 4, 1982, Pope John Paul II told Joseph in Rome that he was appointing him archbishop of Chicago. On July 7 the news was announced in the United States. Virtue, I thought, has been rewarded at least once in history. Joseph, my dear friend Joseph, was going to be what he had long been ready to be.

Chapter 10

THE BISHOP AS GOD'S STEWARD MUST BE BLAMELESS. . . . HE SHOUD BE . . . HOSPITABLE AND A LOVER OF GOODNESS; STEADY, JUST, HOLY AND SELF-CONTROLLED. IN HIS TEACHING HE MUST HOLD FAST TO THE AUTHENTIC MESSAGE, SO THAT HE WILL BE ABLE BOTH TO ENCOURAGE MEN TO FOLLOW SOUND DOCTRINE AND TO REFUTE THOSE WHO CONTRADICT IT.

— TITUS 1:7–10

Summer light filled Holy Name Cathedral as Joseph was installed as Chicago's archbishop by the Vatican's apostolic delegate, Archbishop Pio Laghi, on the afternoon of August 25, 1982. His mother sat in the first row and, as at his ordination as a bishop, had cautioned him about keeping his shoulders straight and not seeming to enjoy himself too much. Sally and I sat just behind his family and it was sweet indeed to witness his assumption of this office if only to rejoice that he had passed through so many trials with such integrity.

I must now admit that I winced when Joseph began his homily with a reference to *E. T.* This is Chicago, I wanted to remind him. Its taste runs to beer more than to gentle fantasy. Before a recent renovation, the cathedral itself bore the scars of a Capone-era mob shoot-out. A lot of the pious faces looking up at you belong to people who could be indicted tomorrow. And the mayor and the governor, the bankers and the businessmen below you are not here for spiritual gain; they're sizing you up, wondering if they can take you or not. I should have had more faith as Joseph gently worked his way, at his own pace and in his own style, to a diplomatic but clear declaration of independence from any particular interest group or center of power in the city.

As I listened, I thought of the surreal and dangerous landscape through which he had made his pilgrimage to this pulpit. He had passed through the equivalent of the once-blood-spattered stockyards without getting a drop on him. Proven wrong were those who said that his career had been doomed by being accidentally cast in the Cody-plot follies. How had he made it through the gauntlet with his integrity unmarred? He knew what was happening, the risks involved, and he understood the almost casual way in which others had involved him in their fancies. The protagonists of these plots and schemes had finally stumbled forth like guests from the stateroom in the classic Marx brothers' movie *A Night at the Opera.*

We had spoken on the phone almost daily during that time of public testing. I was an intimate witness to Joseph's every reaction, to what he was like while the headlines were screaming that he had conspired to overthrow Cody and help rig a papal election. "My priests tell me," he said one evening with wry resignation, "that I couldn't be in on any conspiracy because I would consult with twenty people first." If such moments of self-deprecation were few during those trying days, his true personality was a constant. He had every excuse to be irritated and angry at those who, however inadvertently, had plunged him into the midst of their crisis. In the safe haven of friendship, Joseph remained Joseph. He did not rail against the darkness of this night or criticize anybody else.

I came to understand as I never had before the depths of his fundamental goodness. The public man, often criticized by cynical clergy as ambitious and posturing, was, in fact, the private man as well. Joseph accepted the storm as part of what God asked him to experience as a condition of his service to the Church. He did not understand what Providence was preparing him for—that became clear only many years later—but he made the turmoil the fundament of his spiritual life instead of cursing the unfairness of its focus on him. He began each day now with an hour of prayer, and his calmness flowed from the sure sense he had of giving himself over to God's will, no matter what it was.

If he did not curse, I made up for it on occasion. Joseph might laugh at something I said—that seemed to give him a small measure of relief—but he would never criticize any of the many people who had played fast and loose with his life and reputation. "He's just that way," he would say of someone, "and we have to try to understand him." Or, "I confess that I wish I hadn't been dragged into this, but now I have to take it on as something God wants me to work through." Or he might not say anything at all, restraining himself when he could easily have unloaded a barrage of criticism or self-pity. Joseph might sigh but he would never moan. He was committing himself to the basic premise of his spiritual life: that he must let go rather than cling to anything, even his obvious calling to greater honors and responsibilities in the Church.

Joseph's secretary, Octavie Mosimann—"Tanchie"—first worked for him in Charleston and followed him through Atlanta and Cincinnati to Chicago. She did this, she explained to me and my wife as we sat alone in a parlor of his shadowed residence shortly after he died, "because I didn't want to be away from all that goodness." I understood exactly what she meant. Indeed, by then many around the world did, for they had seen his extraordinary grace in the year of his illness and death. Everybody, I thought, had seen the real Joseph—the only Joseph there was—in his letting go of his life, even as I had seen him, in the prime of his life, spiritually ready to let go of his own plans, his own longings, his legitimate drive to use his gifts as well as he could.

On what I called the "Saturday night massacre," when the first editions of the Chicago papers ran front-page stories about his possible implication in overthrowing Cody, he spoke reflectively but not bitterly about his situation, a man on the lonely mount of that midnight, feeling but not cursing the multiple spiritual deaths of letting go. "I know that there has been a lot of talk about my going to Chicago. And there is a part of me, as you know—I'm not fooling you or myself—

that wants to take on the challenge. But that may not be what God wants. And what looks just right from our view may not be at all what he wants. I've thought today about Archbishop McNicholas, who was here in Cincinnati in the Thirties. He was considered a great leader, and when Patrick Cardinal Hayes of New York died, it was rumored—and he was told—that he would succeed him in New York. Then the pope died and the new one, Pope Pius XII, had been a great friend of an auxiliary bishop of Boston named Spellman. Well, we all know what happened. Spellman went to New York and McNicholas spent the rest of his life in Cincinnati. He never really got the leadership position people thought he was destined for. I want you to know that I am ready to spend the rest of my life here in Cincinnati."

He had let go, as if being purified by a trial of fire, before he could be counted worthy to take the next step, and here, on this day, he had taken it, smiling broadly. No need for any-one to whisper in his ear that all fame is fleeting. His mother would take care of that anyway.

Joseph did look happy, as a man can only on the day before the real work begins, and even a close friend would have been churlish and out of place to remind him, in the slightest way, of any of the adventures of previous months. It seemed right to stay at a certain distance, as John Cardinal Dearden himself did after the liturgical rite had ended in a glorious recessional hymn. Dearden stood between my wife and me on the State Street sidewalk in front of the cathedral. We watched the re-ception line form beneath the striped tent that stretched across the parking lot on the far side of the portion of that famous street that would one day be renamed in Bernardin's honor.

Cardinal Dearden spoke in the tones of a proud father. "I always wanted to see Joe in a great Midwestern diocese like Chicago." Dearden had, of course, been instrumental in getting him into this challenging position. Still, he, who might have stood at Joseph's side and not have been thought out of place, held himself back and, within moments, blended into the swelling crowd around Holy Name, a prince of the Church gracefully letting go of his protégé, leaving him on his own as he made himself invisible.

Dearden's manly self-effacement was an example good enough for us, we decided, so we waited until almost the last in the line of greeters and well-wishers had shaken Joseph's hand. I felt almost as proud as Dearden but somewhat ill at ease, a former priest accompanied by his wife in the midst of clerical festivity, and I did not want to embarrass Joseph or make any kind of claim on his attention or his time. He was beaming as the couples in front of us dwindled down to a precious few. I felt I could not add anything to the recognition that Joseph had deservedly received.

And then, suddenly, we were standing in front of him. Joseph looked directly into my eyes and wordlessly embraced me. My wife, Sally, looked on, smiling at both of us. Joseph embraced her, too, completing the moment, finishing a circle as rounded and true as the rings of our wedding and of his episcopal ordination.

Chapter 11

LOVE ONE ANOTHER

WITH BROTHERLY LOVE . . .

GIVEN TO HOSPITALITY.

— ROMANS 12:10,13

"Look at this," Joseph said, proffering the fine souvenir cup given to him at the civic dinner of welcome held at the Drake Hotel the night before. After the usual boilerplate, the inscription concluded, "Presented to Archbishop Louis Bernardin."

"You now know what the Taste of Chicago means," I said, referring to a popular summer festival.

Joseph laughed heartily, a laugh of letting go in a different way than the New Testament letting go that was the foundation of his spiritual life. This time he was letting go after holding his breath for a long time, making his way like a Wallenda on a tightrope from Cincinnati to Chicago while a blood feud raged below. Now, as the old-priests'-culture phrase put it, he could "put his feet under his own table" again. Words of Irish origin, I thought, out of the mouths of bishops who remained mostly Irish, their eyes still keen for the land their forebears dreamed of every night of their immigrant crossings.

Joseph, the first son of Italian immigrants to be raised to an archdiocese so central in American Catholicism, loved objects more than land, fine things such as the commemorative vessel in his hand, with its classic Chicago low touch of a faulty inscription. Unlike many an Irish or German predecessor who settled for meat and potatoes on the table and lithographs of the Holy Family on the walls, Joseph was comfortable with creation and its fruits, with the subtle and beautiful things he saw as blessings to be cherished. Among these were the paintings and pieces of art whereby he would soon infuse the century-old house with surpassing grace.

Joseph seemed free—suddenly liberated from care, so that he could enjoy without apology what he had hardly let himself think about—conducting Sally and me on a tour of the oak-wooded rooms, warrens, and even the back stairs of this redbrick home, topped with nineteen chimneys, that sat at the very end of State Street on Chicago's North Side. He was having a good time, a boy innocent yet knowing about the good and bad of life. We were carried away by the spirit of this good man who had lived for many years with his mother and sister in public housing in Columbia, South Carolina. Now we were taking delight in *his* taking delight in the house, into which he was breathing life before our eyes.

"This is quite a mansion, at that," I said, using the term common to Chicagoans as we entered his dark-paneled suite of rooms.

"I prefer to call it the *residence*," he replied, revealing his sure sense of the subtle authority of words and of how, even in small ways, he was reframing the image of the archbishopric. He also preferred to call the brick version of Mount Vernon reserved as an archiepiscopal retreat on the grounds of the major seminary at Mundelein the "villa."

Under Cardinal Cody, this big house was a *Flying Dutchman* showing no lights: was anybody aboard, captain or cabin boy, a ghostly crew, perhaps? It was anybody's guess about this vessel of Roman registry foundering on the grassy shore of Lincoln Park. We lived only a few blocks south of it and often walked by its forlorn grounds, untended, unpruned, withered as the biblical fig tree.

Cody had arrived in Chicago with a Vatican I style in 1965, the year that Vatican II ended. Even the enormous good he did, such as funding and supporting the canonical courts that helped people trapped in marriages that had been tragic failures, was not credited to his account, because of his authoritarian style. The unproven accusations that had clouded his last, illness-ridden years made him more reclusive, a man out of due time driven into a melancholy internal exile. His plight was made more poignant by his retention, a few years before, of a public relations firm to improve his image. The results of an early experiment, pictures of him blessing empty body bags at the site of an airplane crash, had been disastrous, obscuring further his humanity.

"You're like Adam, Joe," I said to him, "naming the animals."

He laughed. "Well, we need a fresh start," he replied. "You know that Cody had turned this house into an office building, running fluorescent lights along all these great old ceilings." He shook his head as he pointed upward to the refurbished and repainted areas. "I'm serious when I call this the *residence*. I intend to have other bishops and priests live with me, to entertain here, and even to invite the neighbors in."

Joseph accomplished all these objectives, even though early on some Catholics thought that the house should be sold off to ease archdiocesan finances. It was, Joseph knew, a classic Gospel problem. Some of the apostles had wanted to sell the jar of precious ointment and give the money to the poor. Jesus had better uses for it in anointing his own head. So Joseph transformed an old burden into a vessel of light and warmth to bless the life and work of those who lived under its roof. As Joseph settled in, the grounds shook off their curse and turned a lush green, the bushes came alive, the gardens bloomed, and Catholics were proud that their archbishop lived there.

Joseph was also determined to deal with another issue before the year's end. On December 17, 1982, he planned to release a report on Cardinal Cody's finances, based on available records, done by a professional accounting firm. He was ready to review and close the case on Cody for good. Joseph called about nine-thirty one evening in that month. "I'm meeting the press tonight," he said. "I've just been at a dinner downtown. Roy Larson from the *Sun-Times* was there, and I caught his attention. I told him to come up here with anybody he wanted from that newspaper and I'd answer their questions about Cody's finances."

"Investigative reporters can be bastards," I replied, but he certainly knew this, I understood from his tone, and my reminding him was not really helpful. He was going to do this anyway. Besides, he was telling me, and was not asking for any advice in the matter.

"I know, I know," Joseph said, using the words that he often did to signify that he understood the good and bad side of whatever was under discussion. He was excited, I could tell, that he had fashioned an opportunity to put an end to rumors about Cody, and beyond that, that he was enjoying his new dealings with the press—Earl Bush's principles had been graduate education for his dealing with reporters. Sounding like a fighter anxious for the bell to ring, he promised to call and tell me what had happened.

The session went so late that Joseph did not call me until the next morning. "They were here for over two hours," he said, "and you were right; they became pretty hostile at times. I had to interrupt them and remind them that I was not on trial, that they were my guests.

"I went over the audit. It showed that Cody had spendable receipts of about thirty-eight thousand dollars a year and that his expenditures didn't exceed that. Of course, he didn't keep very good records, but many busy people don't. After everything, I announced, 'I am now bringing this matter to a close.'"

And so he had, for the reporters left, frustrated but convinced that Bernardin was telling them everything he knew. The story was over. Cody was now free from the chain of accusations that had clanked after him into his tomb. He could shed that now and enter eternity. Joseph watched the shadow of his predecessor move away. He had brought Cody peace and a measure of pardon. He also got something he wanted for the new year, 1983: a blank page on which to write his own story.

Our phone rang one brisk early January night. It was Joseph, his voice signaling good news: "The Holy Father is going to hold a consistory soon. I'm one of those who is going to be named a cardinal." The transition was complete. Only a few days more than four months after his installation, Joseph was being given a red hat. This confirmed the Church's confidence in him. It was also the last piece he needed to fashion a new pattern of Church life in Chicago. Cody could rest in even deeper peace. The questions that had floated like the devil's aureole around the title whenever Chicagoans referred to "the cardinal" were dispersed. Now the title belonged to Joseph, who would bring to it as much dignity as he had brought to a house that had seemed as worn out as Cody himself when he had died.

Local reporters never completely converted to referring to his home as the "residence." It did not matter much, although Joseph, in all his years, was careful never to call it anything else. Still, he could smile when I kidded him about it, that half smile of friends in on a secret together.

His residence quickly became a center for some of his most important activity. Before he had been appointed to Chicago, Joseph had been chair of the bishops' committee to draft the pastoral letter on nuclear war. He had immersed himself in this work, conducting many public hearings; among others, Secretary of Defense Caspar Weinberger had given testimony. The first draft had been ready early in 1982. Joseph talked about it often and of the collegial way in which the bishops had carried out this commitment. "It was a test—the first really

important test we've had—of whether we could work together on a major project. So it was the conference itself in the spotlight. And there were some conferences of bishops, especially in Europe, who were taking a close look at us.

"They see us as a country that has never known war firsthand as they have, and the bishops in countries like France and Germany therefore take a slightly different view than we do. They also tend to look at us as a superchurch in a superpower, rich and influential enough to control the agenda. Some others, including plenty of people in Rome, listen to the extremist criticism that we are not loyal to Rome and that we are trying to set up an American Catholic Church."

Joseph was acutely conscious of the risks that the bishops were taking by, in effect, meditating in public on a significant national issue. Later polls indicated not only that their reflections gained the attention of the entire country but that they changed the opinions of many Catholics about the moral acceptability of nuclear war. The Reagan administration had wooed Catholic voters in 1980 and wanted to keep their loyalty during the forthcoming "Morning in America" presidential campaign of 1984. Administration leaders, as Joseph put it, "are uneasy that we bishops are not automatically endorsing their defense buildup. They are also irritated that we have opposed their plans to use force to remove what they consider Communist governments in places like Nicaragua. They are trying to pressure us in various ways to stand down and leave everything to them. There are plenty of Catholics in this administration, and they are deploying them to persuade us. They've got a slogan, 'Take a bishop out to lunch.' "

Joseph was not to be intimidated by the various tactics that critics, whether on the left or on the right, whether from Europe or from the United States, employed to blunt the bishops' theological reflections in the traditional form of a pastoral letter. He was in constant motion in those days, and although we had extensive conversations about this work, many of them were in connection with articles I was writing for *The New York Times Magazine*. They were, therefore, more formal than personal. Still, Joseph did not mind that I, rather than someone else, was translating the bishops' views into print in an influential secular publication.

Joseph was coming into his own, emerging as the Catholic bishops' centrist leader nonpareil, whose picture would appear on the cover of *Time* in 1983, in the spring of which year the letter would appear. Delivering the final draft of the document, called *The Challenge of Peace,* was not easy. The committee, which included former chief of naval chaplains Bishop John O'Connor and peace activist Bishop Thomas Gumbleton, reflected the national ambivalence on the issue. O'Connor (who would be named archbishop of New York in January 1984) did not want to scant the patriotic tradition of American Catholics. Gumbleton wanted to express the convictions of the Catholic peace movement. Joseph convened his group for one last try in late winter at the Friendship Inn in Washington, D.C.

"I felt," Joseph told me on the phone, "that if we could get together and follow our process—let everyone speak until we reached a consensus everybody could live with—we had a chance of pulling it off. It took nine hours, and we made some concessions—such as changing 'halt' to 'curb' concerning the production of nuclear weapons—but as one of them said at the end, we achieved a minor miracle by finishing the document." Even Joseph sounded weary, breathing a sigh as he recounted the bishops' final dialogue on the matter.

Rejecting nuclear war as an unacceptable way of settling differences between nations, the letter's reflections were widely publicized after the bishops adopted it at their meeting in Chicago in May of 1983, Joseph's first full calendar year as the city's archbishop. Later that year he would begin a series of major talks on the "consistent ethic of life," his proposal of a broadened Catholic focus on pro-life issues. If you were for life, you had to oppose abortion, but you also had to link the other issues—some as grave as capital punishment, some less so, such as nutrition programs for infants—that bespoke a commitment to the sanctity of God's gift of life.

By this time, Joseph stood rangy and tall on a national, indeed, an international, stage. His introduction of the consistent ethic of life—sometimes termed the "seamless garment," although he felt the metaphor was misleading because it suggested that all issues were of the same moral importance—confirmed him as the intellectual leader not only of the bishops but of the entire American Catholic community.

I was in regular contact with Joseph during those years, but I was not closely involved in these great works, except as a chronicler of them in newspaper columns, magazine articles, and books. I was also glad to provide background information for other journalists and broadcasters. Despite his necessary travels, Joseph was a growing presence in Chicago, where he was the trusted mediator and *primus inter pares*—first among equals—of its cadre of religious leaders, and a man coming to be recognized by everybody as a gentle pastor to the city at large. I could not escape the feeling that my brother Joseph, already removed, in a sense, to a realm far from the one in which I lived and moved, was destined for something yet greater.

Still, there was one thing that remained a constant, right to the end of his life. Whenever anything occurred that shook or troubled him, he would call me up from wherever he was in the world. I could not provide an answer or wise counsel on issues whose every side he had examined as closely as a diamond cutter examines the jewel beneath his eye. He just wanted to talk freely. It was my unearned and unmerited calling to be his friend as he was mine. It seemed a great grace— a revelation confounding in its implication of me in the mystery of Joseph's life—when, shortly before he died, his oncologist, Dr. Ellen Gaynor, told my wife, "The cardinal always settles down after a visit with your husband."

Chapter 12

HE THAT IS WITHOUT SIN AMONG YOU,

LET HIM CAST THE FIRST STONE.

— JOHN 8:7

Finding blame was never as important to Joseph as uncovering the truth in even the most conflicted situations, in order to resolve them without further harm to anybody involved in them. This was work for a patient miner, ready to dig at levels where the canaries died, far away from the public eye. I sometimes accompanied him on these descents, holding the light or making sure that the rope did not become snarled.

Such an incident occurred in 1986 when, along with *National Catholic Reporter* editor Tom Fox and with the support of others, I became an intermediary between Joseph and Archbishop Raymond Hunthausen of Seattle, Washington—Dutch, as he was called by all of us who knew and loved him. He was a hero to the massive center of moderate Catholics, a pastor whose generosity of heart made him a target for extreme-right-wing Catholic critics. On the basis of their complaints that he was allowing Catholic homosexuals to hold meetings in his cathedral and that he tolerated liturgical variations, Rome investigated and decided, in effect, to transfer his authority to a younger bishop, who would be placed beside him to monitor his behavior.

This episode attracted national publicity and caused immense pastoral unrest among Seattle's Catholics and, indeed, in the central and progressive ranks of Catholics throughout the country. For many weeks, and especially during the November 1986 meeting of the bishops in Washington, Fox and I, joined by Father Richard McBrien of Notre Dame and Father Michael Ryan of Seattle, held together a fragile communications network between Hunthausen, who had been terribly hurt by the incident, and Joseph, the only bishop respected enough to take on the problem when the Seattle archbishop asked his brother bishops to ask for a reconsideration of the case. Tom Fox deserves the credit for sustaining Archbishop Hunthausen through the long months that followed. Joseph had been deputed, along with John Cardinal O'Connor of New York and Archbishop John Quinn of San Francisco, to investigate the situation and to recommend a new solution. With Bernardin's skills and Hunthausen's ultimate readiness to view his exile with the eyes of faith as his share in the redemptive sufferings of Jesus, the situation was righted and Hunthausen's authority was restored by May of 1987.

By then, however, I was seriously ill with the chronic fatigue syndrome, and our contact shifted chiefly to speaking on the phone. As it happened, I was asked by Tom Fox to call Joseph and tell him that Archbishop Hunthausen was ready to work through the last stages of the resolution of the problem. It was about 8 P.M. Chicago time on Tuesday, May 6. "What?" Joseph asked, surprised. "Are you sure about this?"

"Yes. He wanted you and the rest of the commission to know that he is willing to cooperate with you, that he's responding in faith, not to Roman procedures."

"May I say," Joseph responded cautiously, "that I'll believe it when I hear it from him? I've heard things like this before."

"No, this is a triumph, Joe, for the whole collegial process. It's what you've been working for all along, to show that the American Church can take counsel with itself as a Vatican II church."

Joseph accepted my compliments and my interpretation hesitantly. He was not going to relax until the last signature had been blotted on the final agreement. "You're getting like the Irish, Joe," I told him. "The more you succeed, the more you worry." He did manage a laugh, and a few weeks would pass before the matter was settled for good. That was Joseph, however, a worrier in good causes, a worrier about whether he was doing enough, the obsessive who would always hold his breath until the goal was firmly achieved. He would not let go until he was certain that he had invested all his energy and his fine eye for detail into whatever he did.

We still got together regularly. Joseph loved to visit our apartment, sometimes to discuss special problems, such as the sex-abuse scandals among priests, sometimes to have a drink and a good meal. He loved to doff his collar, as he did in many homes in Chicago, and spend an evening after dinner discussing whatever was on his mind. He often asked my wife for psychiatric interpretations of various problems or of individuals with whom he had to deal, always seeking out understandings that would help him be more fair and more helpful to the individuals or groups involved. He also enjoyed talking about his family and learning about ours. One evening he became absorbed in a collection of letters that Sally's father had written to his sister, a nun, about the growth of their family. Joseph laughed heartily as he discovered a reference to a day on which my wife as a little girl had earned no stars for her behavior. He had to be called several times to the dinner table. He chuckled warmly as he asked, "Now, Sally, what exactly did you do that day that you didn't earn any stars?"

In late 1985, he asked us to prepare a memorandum for him on how the bishops might begin to study the problems of priests involved in child abuse. We did this, and Joseph submitted it as a proposal to the then–conference general secretary, Monsignor Daniel Hoye. It was Joseph's hope that this could be the beginning of a new intensive study of the priesthood. But Monsignor Hoye, after consulting with some of the members of the committee concerned with priestly life, returned the memorandum, suggesting, in a brief, mildly cryptic response, that he would not send it to the bishops in general because he did not think they would do anything as a group about the issue. This almost willful ignorance motivated Joseph to begin the development of guidelines for dealing with accusations of sex abuses by church workers in the archdiocese of Chicago.

These many evenings seem precious now in remembrance, a rosary of good times while I waited, sure that everything we had witnessed in Joseph's life and work was but prologue to a greater challenge, forming itself beyond our view, its first seeds coming into being as little noticed as the pinprick low at the far end of the weather map just coiling its energies together for a storm nobody has yet predicted or even suspected.

Joseph was being prepared for something—I had that part right and used to joke with him about it—but nobody could then grasp his true destiny: to be caught up in the mystery of suffering, death, and resurrection that he had preached and tried to live more intensely every day of his life.

Chapter 13

I TELL YOU SOLEMNLY, AS A YOUNG MAN
YOU FASTENED YOUR BELT AND WENT ABOUT AS YOU
PLEASED; BUT WHEN YOU ARE OLDER YOU WILL
STRETCH OUT YOUR HANDS, AND ANOTHER WILL TIE
YOU FAST AND CARRY YOU OFF AGAINST YOUR WILL.

*JESUS TO PETER AFTER
TELLING HIM, "FEED MY SHEEP"*
— JOHN 21:18

"Is it possible," a questioner asked me after a lecture at Chatauqua in the summer of 1989, "that we will ever have an American pope?"

In the few seconds I paused, Joseph's face rose in my imagination. Yes, I said, I think it is possible that Cardinal Bernardin of Chicago could be elected pope. He is richly qualified for the position and few in the history of the Church have been better prepared by nature and grace. As I walked back to the cottage in which I was staying, images of Joseph presented themselves spontaneously, cascading as transparent sheets of water do over a rocky ledge.

I saw Joseph, his forehead wrinkled with concern as he talked of the criticism he had received, some from priests, some quite violent, when he was faced with closing a number of parishes and schools that sat nearly as empty as abandoned forts in changed neighborhoods across the city. He had read to me excerpts from a priest's letter: " 'You are no better than your predecessor. Your staff won't tell you, your priests won't tell you. . . . Undo all this.' "

Joseph had been upset by the character of such letters; surely people must understand that we cannot support every parish and every school, that we must consolidate in order to continue educating at all. Still, it was one of the most difficult periods for him because some attributed motives to him that he was constitutionally incapable of experiencing—smallness, spite, disregard of the feelings of others.

On such occasions, I recalled, I had been able to offer a small service to Joseph. I wrote a column for the *Chicago Tribune* that an editor gracefully entitled "That the Church May Be More Than a Memory in Chicago." I argued that Joseph was not trying to destroy a treasured past but to guarantee that the Church would have a future in which to serve and educate new generations, especially of the poor. It appeared on the morning he was to meet with a large number of priests on the issue. It offered a different way of looking at the situation. Joseph was buoyed by it, and later, many priests were kind enough to thank me for writing it.

Joseph was thankful in complete harmony with the way

we were friends. We knew each other's moves and timing and what each would or should carry in difficult times. He did not have to say much and I did not have to hear anything to know that I had done the right thing. We never thought that doing what we should do merited celebration.

I could hear Joseph's voice reading me the compromise phrasing that he had worked at late at night to resolve an impasse among the bishops on their 1987 pastoral letter, *The Many Faces of AIDS: A Gospel Response.* Halfway through its thirty pages, which urged Catholics to understand AIDS as a "human disease," the document acknowledged that in a pluralistic society, some groups counseled the use of condoms to prevent the illness. The relevant paragraph concluded that the bishops were not "promoting the use of prophylactics but merely providing information that is part of the factual picture."

About thirty bishops protested including such a reference, and the bishops' conference was soon in turmoil over the matter. As their June meeting approached, some observers felt that the conference could be shipwrecked on the reef of this issue. "First of all," Joseph told me, "I'm going to tell them that the future of our work together is at stake, that we cannot withdraw the document without giving the impression that the whole thing is flawed. We cannot go on arguing this thing. I'm going to propose that we let this document stand as it is and that we draft another one that will allow for clarifications that some of the bishops want to make."

He called me again after his presentation at the bishops' June meeting in 1988. "I told them no solution was perfect, but this would guarantee the bishops' ability to work together. It was very quiet when I finished. Then Bernie seconded my approach and it passed unanimously." "Bernie" was Bernard Cardinal Law of Boston, who had raised questions about the first draft. Joseph sounded relieved, proud, weary. "On the way out, one of the bishops said to me, 'You've saved the conference.' I certainly hope so."

Because he had resolved this potentially damaging crisis in such a skillful way, Joseph seemed to be emerging even more strongly as a candidate for the papacy, someone his fellow cardinals, like his fellow bishops, counted a man of deep faith, who listened fully to all sides of a question before making a decision. He possessed, far more than any other American prelate, a characteristic that could never be claimed but only earned, and then awarded spontaneously by his colleagues: credibility.

I recalled Joseph's voice again on the phone. He was sending over a copy of a document he had been working on ever since he was unable to get the bishops to address the problem of pedophilia among priests. "We're going to have a process to be followed when accusations are made against any Church worker, priest or layman. There will be a fitness review board to examine the allegations. They'll be able to make real decisions about whether the accused person should be removed from their work while the charges are investigated."

The red-covered document was delivered that evening. It was classic Joseph: carefully worked-out policy, fruit of and offering to the obsessive gods of bureaucracy. But then, as I said to him later, it was designed to allow a specific bureaucracy to react to charges of sexual abuse that were often lost or long delayed in other bureaucratic institutions. He sounded pleased that he finally had the process in place, pleased as only he could sound after coming out of hundreds of hours of consultations and drafts with exactly the document he wanted.

His voice sounded different, pressured but calm, with a faint halo of the anxiety he was keeping in check. "I've got something I have to talk to you about." I reached for a yellow note pad, wrote down the date and time: *11/11/93, 5:19 P.M.* "I've got John O'Malley, my legal counsel, here. We've been going over information that's been coming in here in bits and pieces. It appears that I am going to be named as a defendant in a sex-abuse case that will be filed tomorrow."

My own hand quivered slightly as I began to write. I had received calls from newspaper reporters over the past hour asking if I knew anything about a big story about to break concerning a high-ranking American church leader. Tom Roberts, a good friend from Religious News Service in New York, got right to the point: Did I think it was *remotely* possible that there could be anything in charges of sex abuse against Cardinal Bernardin? Not a chance, I said. He has lived in public all his life, there is no difference between his public and private lives. Roberts agreed, but I could hear in his and other callers' voices the sound of a big story revving up.

Now Joseph was telling me what he knew about a "preposterous story that I haven't got any connection with." The charges had not yet been delivered to him, but Mary Ann Ahern, a reporter on the local NBC affiliate, had obtained excerpts and read them over the phone to the cardinal. The plaintiff was a thirty-four-year-old man named Steven Cook who had once been a seminarian in Cincinnati. The suit had been filed by a lawyer named Rubino; he claimed to have lots of evidence, including pictures.

"This whole thing came about," Joseph explained, "in the last couple of weeks. My name was added to a case in Cincinnati against a Father Ellis Harsham. He supposedly abused Steven Cook when he was a student at the high school seminary."

Joseph paused. His tone turned close to exasperation as he referred to his successor in Cincinnati, Archbishop Dan Pilarczyk. "Dan and his chancellor, a priest named Conlon, have been driving this case. Dan claims that this Steven Cook's lawyer is bluffing, that he is 'just fishing,' and nothing is going to happen. This Father Harsham may have had a relationship with Cook, but Conlon has rebuffed the lawyer with a letter that almost dares him to sue. I talked to Pilarczyk an hour ago. He insists that nothing will happen."

"Dan is pretty arrogant at times," I said.

Joseph let me make the judgment as he continued. "Apparently this poor young man, Cook—and I have a feeling that he is being used in this—feels that he was ruined by this experience, that he became a male prostitute, that he's been forced to be a sexual actor hundreds, if not thousands, of times. Now, I'm told, he is very ill with AIDS, that he is dying."

How, I asked, did Joseph's name get into this? He did not have the slightest idea, he could not recall the young man at all, he wasn't going to dignify this charge with any kind of response. This whole thing was absurd—how could he defend himself against something that never happened?

John O'Malley, the lean classic black Irishman who was the diocesan attorney, got on the phone. A composed man, he would have remained cool midst the gunfire at the O.K. Corral. A good man for the moment, I judged. The cardinal should issue at least a simple statement of denial; what did I think? Let Joseph do it in his own words, as few as possible. O'Malley agreed. Joseph got back on the phone.

"As far as I can learn, the charges against me came to this young man in a dream. Some kind of memory supposedly came back to him." He paused. I could see, without a picture phone, his liquid brown eyes searching mine—the gaze of an old friend—from behind his outsize glasses. "You've known me a long time. *You* know that I could never have done anything like this."

You? Not a chance, I affirmed. Only somebody who doesn't know you could believe this, I told him, mentally searching through the files of the years for a contrary tab. No, Joseph's life has always been too public, too forthcoming, too scheduled, too restrained and controlled; he was too good, for God's sake, to break the commandments in this way.

Plenty of people were ready to believe bad news about anybody, Joseph responded. "This is the worst kind of charge they can make against me. The only thing I really have going for me as the pastor of this local church of Chicago is my credibility, that our people trust me. This accusation aims right at that. If people can't trust me, then I can't be their bishop."

In short, his whole life and work were on the line. The story was crackling on the wires already and would be the only thing some people would ever hear or read about him. Bernardin? Oh yes, wasn't he the one who abused one of his seminarians?

Joseph was upset that the accusation had filtered across the world while he had not seen the complaint yet. Besides that,

CNN had just called to get his public schedule for tomorrow. They wanted to ambush him with a camera someplace. They were already running promotional bits about a special on clerical sex abuse to run on Sunday night, the eve of the annual bishops' meeting in Washington, D.C.

Joseph had looked out his office window at the television news trucks assembling below on Superior Street. They were shouldering one another like animals to get better feeding positions. He sat down and wrote out a brief statement to be issued immediately. He read it to me over the phone: "While I have not seen the suit and do not know the details of the allegation, there is one thing I do know, and I state categorically: I have never abused anyone in all my life, anywhere, anytime, anyplace."

After we hung up, I sat for a while thinking about my friend Joseph, indeed, my brother Joseph. Nothing could be less possible and nothing could hurt him more than the public mugging of this sordid accusation, this lightning strike out of a sunny sky to his heart and soul, to the self he presented to the world every day, the man who was exactly the same on camera as he was off. The telephone rang and shook me out of my ruminations, my fear, deep as Victoria Falls, that the finest man I knew could be destroyed, the good he had done shattered, his future obliterated by this attack. It was the novelist John Gregory Dunne calling from New York, a soul mate of a different kind, expressing support at exactly the right moment. Nobody who knows of your friend Joe will believe this for a minute.

His words bolstered me for a stream of calls from various television and newspaper reporters, most of whom were sympathetic to Joseph—but what could this be all about anyway? Where there's smoke, there may be fire. Is there *any* chance—do you think this just *might* have happened?

No way.

Information also comes in about Steven Rubino, the lawyer from Ventnor, New Jersey, who is filing the suit in the morning. He has sued priests for sexual abuse before and has developed something of a reputation for it. A zealot, some say, and a do-gooder whose judgment has come into question since he recently sued the entire diocese of Camden, New Jersey, on the basis of the organized crime law, the famous RICO statute. A rogue priest, Charles Fiore, who has denounced Joseph many times in the extremist Catholic paper the *Wanderer,* out of St. Paul, Minnesota, has involved himself in what he has apparently styled an opportunity "to get" Cardinal Bernardin.

Bill Kurtis, then anchor of the CBS affiliate in Chicago, calls just before he goes on the air at ten o'clock. His news judgment tells him that something doesn't fit together, and on the air, he boldly raises the question of whether there is some calculation in the attack on Joseph, some enthusiasm for this assault by people who dislike him. God bless you, Bill, I thought before battling through a ten-round bout of sleeplessness that ended when I got up around five-thirty the next morning.

Joseph, however, had arisen even earlier and spent his first hour, as usual, in prayer. "It came clear to me," he said on a call before breakfast, "what I have to do in this situation. I have to trust in God, who has allowed this for some purpose, and I have to put my trust in the truth. Jesus says in the Gospels that the truth will make us free. I believe that with all my heart." At times of stress, Joseph's Southern accent surfaced lightly, so "believe" was softly truncated into "b'lieve." That sound touched me like the gap-toothed smile in a child's photograph, for it contained the essence of his innocence, his forthrightness, the goodness of that boy in him who never went bad. Yet he was at his manliest. He had prayed to the Lord and was ready to meet the noonday devil. He was having a press conference at 1 P.M.

Calls from the media began at seven-fifteen. A camera crew from the local Fox television station arrived. The city bubbled like a cauldron. At midmorning a copy of the complaint clattered out of the fax machine. Written in the classic assaultive language of the trial lawyer, its objective was to shake the person named as defendant rather than uncover the truth. It was filed that day, November 12, 1993, in the United States District Court, Southern District of Ohio, Western Division, #0-1-93-0784, and signed off on for Rubino by a Cincinnati lawyer named Andrew Lipton. Paragraph 21 noted that "beginning in October 1993, plaintiff Steven Cook began to recall sexual abuse committed against him by defendant Bernardin while plaintiff was a minor."

Ten minutes before his scheduled press conference at one o'clock, Joseph called and told me how the complaint had been reviewed in the archdiocesan conference room that morning. Joseph sat at the head of a table ringed by his cabinet of priest advisers as well as a group of lawyers and public relations experts who had offered their services in the crisis. They had come to paragraph 22, which described the asserted abuse. After the plaintiff had been brought to the archbishop's room in the old-fashioned residence where I had visited him so many years before, Bernardin was said to have engaged in acts that included "kissing, fondling of the male genitals and buttocks, culminating in Steven Cook's being sodomized." Joseph slammed his fist on the conference table. "That's where they've gone too far. *Nobody* who knows me will ever believe I did those things to anybody."

Joseph had listened then to the advice of the aides and experts arrayed tensely around him. In general, the priests counseled him to follow his own instincts. The others proposed a variety of tactics, depending on the possible changes in the situation—when to speak, when to deny, when to let the lawyers speak, and so forth. "I took it all in," Joseph said calmly, "then I went to my office to be alone for a while. I prayed again and thought things over. And now I've made up my mind." I could feel the enormous resolve in him, the coalescence and concentration of his best energies, which, although swaddled in gentleness, constituted a force of which enemies would wisely take careful measure before advancing on him.

"I've heard what I shouldn't do and what I ought to do. I listened to it all." Joseph's voice was clear and determined; he had made up his own mind. "But I'm going to take charge of this thing myself. I'm not following any strategies. I'm just going to tell the truth, the simple truth. Those that don't like it can go to hell."

Joseph was not worried about public relations or legal tactics. Those were foreign tongues to him. For him—it was obvious to me—this was a spiritual matter. He had to let go of earthly support systems. He had to loosen his grip on everything, jump into a free fall, tumbling down through the blue, sustained by his faith in the Lord.

Joseph was self-possessed as he went downstairs, armed only with his own integrity, to meet the seventy and more journalists who stirred and chatted nervously while cameramen and sound technicians wearing leather jackets and reversed baseball caps dragged cables across the floor and adjusted the camera to televise the event.

I held my breath, found myself too restless to sit down in front of my television set as Joseph, followed by his auxiliary bishops and other black-suited aides, entered the large room set aside for the conference. Joseph, surrounded, seemed alone, for the escort that had seen him to this place now stepped back. He was on his own and he knew it. This was not unlike entering an arena on the highest pagan feast day. The beasts pawing the sand had been denied food that they might be the more ravenous.

The shouted questions overlapped one another until Joseph's dignity slowed them down; he began to answer every inquiry fully and without defensiveness. No, he had not abused anybody, and no, he could not remember Steven Cook, and yes, he had submitted the accusations against himself to the very review board on sexual abuse he had set up earlier that fall, for their study and recommendations. Yet he answered so gently and so peacefully that the atmosphere in the room began to change. He had grounded the loose electrical charge, and gradually the reporters, hardened to a hundred denials a day from politicians, developers, lawyers, and landlords, understood that Joseph was doing something against the grain of America's experience with public figures or celebrities caught up in scandal—Joseph was telling the truth, and the truth, as he had trusted, was setting him free.

The mood was thoroughly transformed by the time the questions trailed off. As one veteran reporter was to tell me later, "I wished I could just take him in my arms and say, 'Don't worry, Cardinal, everything is going to be all right.' "

Still, there was one last question tipped with poison. It came from a young reporter at the edge of the crowd—one last test of the mettle of the man before them. If he could handle this question gracefully, nobody there would think him anything but innocent of the charges.

"Are you," the young man asked, "sexually active?"

Joseph paused. The room went silent as the television does when the lines go down. You didn't know how loud it had been until it stopped. Joseph looked benevolently at the journalist and spoke as gently as he might to a penitent in the confessional. "I have always lived a chaste and celibate life," he said. The hostility in the news conference was immediately diluted. Joseph had done it as Jesus must have, I thought, when he walked away through the once-angry crowd and no one wished to harm him. Tears formed in my eyes as I watched him turn and head through the door to the next phase of this ordeal. It was not long in coming.

CNN had been running teasers all day that featured excerpts from an interview made weeks earlier between reporter Bonnie Anderson and an angry Steven Cook. The bold journalist and the angry plaintiff were shown examining what could not be seen very well, supposed evidence—pictures of Steven and the cardinal together, a signed book, a picture given as a gift. Steven spoke grimly of the man he had accused of abusing him sexually. Nothing would suit him except Bernardin's removal from his office for all the harm he had done. It was powerful television. *See the whole interview on Sunday night, nine o'clock Eastern Time.*

I talked to Joseph after the press conference. I told him that he had broken the back of the dragon, that the press was all on his side, that any doubts they had—any doubts viewers had—had been transformed by the power of the truth. He was glad to hear that, and then he asked me if I had seen any of the CNN promos. "This is disgusting," he said. "They interviewed me some months ago about the program I was developing for Church personnel accused of sexual abuse. Now they are tacking this interview with Steven Cook onto it and making it seem an exposé of me. And it can't be an accident that it's showing on the night before the bishops open their meeting in Washington."

He was going ahead with his plans to attend the meeting, and he would meet the press anywhere, anytime. Bernard Cardinal Gantin, head of the Roman congregation that appointed bishops, had called him and offered his full support. So had the American archbishop Justin Rigali, of the Vatican diplomatic academy, saying that everybody in Rome was standing with him. These words from the Vatican were very important to Joseph, who still felt that it was difficult to defend himself in these circumstances. "I won't say anything critical of Steven Cook," he said, "because I have an idea that he's being used, that he is as much a victim as anybody in this. I've decided to write him a personal letter. The lawyers tell me that I have to send it to him through this Rubino. But I want him to know that I feel for him."

Joseph went to Washington with his youthful but accomplished and devoted executive assistant, Father Kenneth Velo, and we kept in touch throughout the days of the gathering. The bishops had given him a standing ovation, and Joseph had held another press conference similar to the one he had in Chicago, answering every question undefensively, hacking free of the growth of entangling inquiries with the sharp single-edged blade of truth. Back in Chicago, the outlandish priest Fiore, who had attacked him regularly in the extremist press, had appeared on a local radio talk show, claiming that he had been watching Bernardin a long time and was glad that he had been charged at last. Yes, he believed the charges, and, yes, he knew Steven Cook, he boasted, he had talked to him several times and he had talked to his mother, too, on more than one occasion.

Let me pause in this narrative to offer, from sources as different as Steven Cook's mother, Mary, and his companion of nine years and caregiver, Kevin Nealey, the elusive truth about the self-promoting figure of Fiore, so like an eccentric attaching himself to a murder case with empty promises of evidence. A priest in the process of being ousted from the Dominican order, Fiore had for years directed his family business, Fiore Properties, from a $600,000 home near Madison, Wisconsin. He had been in constant trouble with superiors but had attempted to make himself an expert on clerical sexual abusers, associating them with satanism. Learning of the charges against Bernardin, he attempted to expand his brief onetime appearance as an adviser to lawyer Steven Rubino and one conversation with the plaintiff into a role of central significance. Ordered to appear for a deposition in February

1994, he claimed he had a heart attack and disappeared, discredited, into the crowd.

On November 23, 1993, Chuck Goudy, a reporter for the ABC affiliate in Chicago, began filing stories about the use of hypnosis on Steven Cook to help him recover memories of the sexual abuse by then Archbishop Bernardin. Skepticism was surfacing about the procedure and the young woman who carried it out, as well as the psychologist who had allegedly supervised the procedure. The case had been presented sensationally to the nation and the world through the questionable exclusive deal that CNN had worked out in advance of the filing. Nonetheless, Rubino kept saying that he had plenty of evidence, that the charges were as solid as a fortress. Slowly but surely, however, it was beginning to look, to Joseph's lawyers John O'Malley and James Serritella, like a one-dimensional movie set with little behind it.

Joseph relied on his lawyers for the technical pursuit of the case but had thrown himself completely into the matter as well. While he was encouraged by the news that the charges were beginning to come apart, he understood that the protocol of the civil justice system had to be followed. Justice moved slowly, and although he was told that it was unlikely that he would ever have to go to trial, Joseph told me and my wife, "I wake up in the middle of the night and I am seated in the witness box as all these spurious accusations are made over and over again." He was calm, but to anybody close to him, it was clear that the false charges had hit him hard, had wounded him in his soul and spirit. My wife, who had written a book about going through a trial for medical malpractice, understood what Joseph was experiencing very well. She talked to him regularly and sent him her book, *Defendant,* to help him deal with the psychological impact of being accused of violating your deepest values and commitments.

Joseph had submitted his case to the archdiocesan fitness review board, and on December 7, the board received a letter apparently prepared for Steven Cook's signature by his lawyer. In it, Cook refused to meet with the board and sharply criticized the system of dealing with sex-abuse cases. "I'm not going to read his letter," Joseph told me, "so I won't have any comments about it." He had been at Saint Agatha's Church, a black parish on the West Side, the previous night. "They sang a special hymn for me," he said—" 'This Trouble Will Not Last Forever.' That was *really* very nice."

Everywhere he went, he received standing ovations of support. And every day some new information came through showing that the charges were imploding, that Rubino had obviously hurried his case together sloppily, that it would soon collapse completely from within. Andrew Lipton, the Cincinnati lawyer who had signed off on the complaint for that Southern Ohio jurisdiction, had become suspicious of its character and had begun to talk with—indeed, virtually to work for—Bernardin's attorneys.

Still, Joseph bore a hurt that would not easily heal within him, no matter how flimsy the case was. Some commentators even said that, should Bernardin be vindicated, as seemed likely, he would be forever notorious, that the outline of the stain, like that of a stain cleansed from a wall long ago, would still be seen for years. He smiled when he heard encouraging news, but it was often a tight smile, stretched over a soul that, assaulted in its finest point with such unspeakable accusations, would ache permanently. The accusers, even should they be shown as frivolous, had already accomplished part of their objective. The torch of shaming had reached inside the walls and lay there, smoldering still.

Deeper things were on Joseph's mind. One of them was Steven Cook himself. The more he learned, the more Joseph was convinced that this young man, who may well, he thought, have been abused by the Father Harsham named in the complaint, had been abused again by the lawyers who had jerry-rigged this case. On November 20, Joseph had written in longhand, in his trademark Palmer penmanship, a letter to the young man. He gave me a copy of it to read:

Dear Steven,

Needless to say, I was shocked and hurt by the allegation you made against me. I was shocked because I have never abused any-one in all my life.

But as I thought it over, I began to think that you must be suf-fering a great deal. The idea came to me yesterday morning that it would be a good thing if I visited with you personally. The pur-pose of the visit would be strictly pastoral—to show my concern for you and to pray with you.

If you are interested in such a visit, please let me know. I will come to you if you wish.

> *Sincerely yours in Christ,*
> *Joseph Card. Bernardin*
> *Archbishop of Chicago*

Not until months later did Joseph learn that Rubino never delivered the letter, sent Federal Express to his care that day.

Meanwhile, O'Malley, Serritella, and the other lawyers were methodically dismantling what was turning out to be a tottering edifice. But such structures must be taken down carefully, the lawyers decided, lest they collapse halfway through the process, obliterating the tale their old bricks tell to those who know how to listen to them. The evidence that CNN had touted so highly and that Bonnie Anderson had gazed at so knowingly turned out to lack any of the character and quality of real evidence. The picture that they implied revealed Joseph in a compromising situation with the plaintiff turned out to be a group photo taken at the Cincinnati seminary on some ceremonial occasion. Steven was on one side of the crowded scene, Joseph was on the other. The book supposedly autographed by Joseph bore no man's autograph and apparently had come from the library of a deceased bishop from the Covington diocese, across the Ohio River. The picture allegedly given as a gift was a loose advertising piece resembling those routinely mailed to sell books and recordings.

Fiore's checkered ecclesiastical record, replete with evidence of his being removed from various assignments in questionable circumstances, read like a Postal Service notice about a confidence man. The hypnotist, a woman named Michelle Moul, had no qualification, license, or professional training to carry out sessions in which memories were supposedly recovered. Listed by Rubino as an expert, she freely admitted that she was not one and that she was horrified that what she had done with Steven Cook had become the basis for a suit against anyone, much less Cardinal Bernardin.

Moul had been drawn into the case at the suggestion of a woman who worked for Rubino. Apparently, this woman, a paralegal, as Steven Cook's mother recalls, had been the source for suggesting that the name Bernardin be proposed to Steven Cook during this alleged episode of recovering a lost memory. He did not mention Joseph then but, confusedly, later on in a conversation that he supposedly had with a friend. Cook's lawyers admitted that the hypnotist might have skewed the results of the session. In February 1994 Dr. William C. Wester Jr., an expert on hypnotism who had worked with Steven Cook when he was in the seminary, would examine the plaintiff, who readily admitted that he could not remember anything about the charges he had made. Nonetheless, the lawyers and the court had to follow a careful process. On February 28, 1994, 108 days after they were filed, Steven recanted the charges he had made against Joseph.

Joseph stepped before microphones in Chicago and uttered a simple, heartfelt phrase, *"Deo gratias,"* thanks be to God. That week *ABC Evening News* named him the Man of the Week. I was interviewed for the segment but only one sentence was broadcast, the one in which I said that Joseph was well qualified to become the pope someday.

On February 27, the day before the recantation, Rubino tried to alter the conditions that had been worked out and Joseph told his lawyers that he would seek sanctions if these were not dropped. It was then that Joseph told me of how the impact of the event was catching up with him. "I feel a very deep emotion building in me," he said, half surprised, yet not so surprised at that. I am human, he seemed to be saying, I am beginning to feel everything I've been through here, as if the greatness of the relief were the measure of the hardness of the test. "I have never felt anything quite this way before."

The light was filtered at best during the three months that intervened between accusation and recantation. Despite the impact of Joseph's honesty in dealing with the matter, newspapers and television news operations sent reporters all over the country to unearth or to track down any possible scandal about Joseph. He was rumored, for example, to have had an affair with a florist in Atlanta, but this was nonsense, as were all the other false leads. *Vanity Fair* commissioned Jason Berry, a highly respected reporter who had been the first to expose priests involved in pedophilia in the South, to write a piece about the case against Joseph. The magazine ultimately rejected the piece because they felt that he was innocent, but its very commission was a measure of the heightened reportorial atmosphere at the time. Later, Joseph could smile, at least a bit, when I told him that he was probably the most investigated man in America, and the man with the cleanest slate—nobody had been able to find anything against him.

It had been a searing experience. Why, I wondered, as did Joseph, had this happened? What did God have in mind? He's preparing you for something else, I told Joseph, and he would nod, but he seemed to be thinking deep thoughts himself.

The stress of the period was never more evident than when Joseph came for his Christmas season dinner, on Sunday, December 12, 1993. He had taken off his collar and slipped into a white cashmere sweater that he had brought with him. A reflective mood held us all as we talked before and during dinner. Joseph spoke of how kind the people had been, of how heartening it was when strangers approached to express their confidence in him, or when truckers leaned out of their cabs to give him the thumbs-up sign. He sat afterward in our living room, sipping a Grand Marnier from a Waterford glass. Dear Joseph, how gentle you are and how hurt you have been.

He stayed much later than usual, speaking mostly about the case, talking to Sally about how right she had been in her description of what happens to you internally, beneath the reach of anybody, however close, to touch or give, when you are falsely accused—how alone you feel and how much you must rely on the Lord. Near 11 P.M., he donned his collar and his suit coat, then his overcoat, and paused, standing in our foyer.

He beckoned Sally and me to step closer, reached out, and put his arms around us so that we three stood as one, face-to-face in the cone of light from the fixture above. "I want you to know," Joseph said softly, "that of all my friendships, this is the most important." We held together for a moment and he gently pulled his arms away from us. In the cold, dark night we drove him home the few blocks to his residence, blazing with Christmas lights. There was no need for any of us to say anything as we watched him unlock the front door and step inside.

Chapter 14

To me . . . was given the grace

to preach . . . the unfathomable riches of

Christ and to enlighten all men on the

mysterious design which for ages was

hidden in God, the Creator of all.

— Ephesians 3:8–9

I used to remember June 6 because it is the anniversary of D-Day, in 1944. Now I remember it because of what happened on that date, a Tuesday, in 1995. A summerlike day was gallantly holding off evening when the doorman called to say, "Cardinal's on his way up."

Joseph had said he wanted to stop in around 5 P.M. Will Sally be there?

No, she's in Cincinnati examining candidates for their board certification. She should be in around six-thirty.

Fine, he had said, and here he was standing at the open

door. He looked wonderful, dressed in a good suit, a half an inch of white cuff showing. Would you make me a Manhattan on the rocks, Canadian Club, if you have it?

I don't make them as well as Sally does for you, I said, but I'll try.

He settled into his favorite place on the couch, where, through the large living room windows, he could look out on Lake Michigan, smooth as artificial turf, and toward the gentle curve of East Lake Shore Drive and Navy Pier beyond. He sipped the drink—not bad, he complimented me with a smile.

"You know, Gene," he said comfortably, "it's been quite a year and a half. The false accusation, of course, then the recantation by Steven Cook. The one thing I always wanted, to finish that experience, was the chance to meet him and reconcile with him. And I got that last Christmas."

He recreated the scene briefly. He and Father Scott Donahue had flown to Philadelphia on December 30, 1994, rented a car, and driven out to the St. Charles Borromeo seminary in the suburb of Overbrook. The ragged ermine of hard, dying snow lay along the curbs and circles.

"You know how empty and cold seminaries can be during vacation time. Well, the rector met us at the main building and escorted us to a large room on the second floor, and I wondered if Steven would really come. Finally we heard a car, and in a few minutes Steven came in with his friend and caregiver, Kevin Nealey.

"He seemed a little ill at ease—I suppose we all were—and I told him that I had come to put an end to everything we had been through. I told him that I knew that there were many influences on him at the time but that I had no ill feelings toward him, none at all, and that I hoped we might just meet and perhaps pray together for his physical and spiritual well-being.

"At first he hesitated, then he told me that he had wanted to meet me and apologize to me for all the embarrassment and hurt he felt that he had caused me a year before. But he also wanted to tell me about his life. He was very bitter about being seduced by a faculty member in the seminary. When he complained to the authorities, they hadn't believed him. He became estranged from the Church after that. Often, when he was in a hotel room, he would throw the Gideon Bible against the wall to express his anger at all organized religion.

"He explained that he had come in contact with the lawyer Rubino to file a suit against the priest who had abused him in the seminary. He seemed confused and uncertain as to exactly what happened when he went to the alleged hypnotist or how he got the idea—or the recovered memory—of my abusing him. His companion broke in to say that he never trusted or liked Rubino or the priest Fiore, who telephoned him once at the lawyer's behest.

"I looked Steven directly in the eyes and I said, 'You know that I never abused you.' Steven replied, 'I know.' Then he paused and asked if I could tell him that again. 'I never abused you,' I said. 'You know that, don't you?' And Steven nodded and said, 'Yes, I know that and I want to apologize for saying that you did.'

"I was happy to accept his apology, of course, and assured him of my prayers, and then asked him if he would like me to say Mass for him. Steven hesitated. 'I'm not sure I want to have Mass. I've been alienated from God and the Church for a long time. Maybe a simple prayer would be more appropriate.'

"So I opened my case and asked if he would like to have the gifts I had brought. One was a book of the Gospels I had inscribed for him, but I told him I'd understand if he didn't want to take it. But then his eyes welled with tears and he took the Gospels and pressed them against his heart. Then I took a hundred-year-old chalice out and told him I had received it from a man I didn't even know. All he asked was that I say Mass for Steven someday.

"Steven smiled and he said, 'Please, let's celebrate Mass now.' So we all went to the chapel, and Kevin said he wasn't Catholic, and should he participate? Of course, I said, and the four of us had Mass, and I anointed Steven afterward. It was a great moment, believe me. Then I said a few words about how in every family there are times of hurt and anger or alienation but that we can't run away from our family. After every falling out, we must make every effort to be reconciled. So, too, the Church, I told him, is our spiritual family. We may become hurt or alienated, but it is still our family. Since there isn't any other, we must work at reconciliation. And I told him that that is what we had been doing that afternoon. Before he left, Steven told me that a big burden had been lifted from him. He felt healed and very much at peace."

In the silence that followed, I said, "Well, Joe, you were really the Good Shepherd."

His eyes questioned me above his drink. He seemed on the verge of a blush.

"Well, you went after the one sheep that had gone astray and left the other ninety-nine of us back here in Chicago."

"No, no," he cut in, making the Manhattan sway gently in the half arc he described with his glass to suggest the measure by which I was off target. "I just did what a good pastor should do. And despite everything, I couldn't believe that Steven was a lost sheep or a big sinner. He was sinned against far more than he sinned."

Joseph steadied his glass, sipped from it appreciatively. "What I wanted to talk about was whether I should ever write this up, or have you write it up. But I think now, especially with the reconciliation with Steven, and the charges resolved, that I would rather put it all behind me. I'm anxious to get on to the future. I want this all to be in the past."

"Then that is exactly what you should do," I replied.

Joseph visibly relaxed. Do you really think so?

Of course. Your healthy Italian feelings are telling you which way to go. Don't ever go against them.

He looked me in the eye as he raised his glass as if in a toast. "We've been through a lot together," he said. "Maybe things will be easier in the future." He smiled, gestured toward the gaudy neon-trimmed Ferris wheel that was slowly turning against the blue-black sky at Navy Pier. "If you'll go for a ride on that," he said playfully, "I'll go with you."

He began to talk about a range of matters on his mind, the chief of which was his disagreement with the new Republican Congress and its members' idea that private charities, such as the Church, could take over for the programs that they were cutting out. He had almost finished his drink when the phone rang and I went into the kitchen to answer it.

It was my wife, calling from Cincinnati. A string of thunderstorms was causing flight delays. She would be home much later than she expected.

"Is that Sally?" Joseph called from the living room. "I want to talk to her." He came into the kitchen, took the phone, and I returned to the living room. I couldn't hear what he was saying.

He returned in a few minutes. The image of him in that moment is fixed forever in my album of memory. He looked so healthy, so well tailored, so fit for the challenges ahead. It is a portrait of a man at the top of his form, a man free now to plunge as pilgrims do into what, for him, were the healing waters of work. It is Joseph catching the first light on the summit of the craggy and dangerous mountain he had just climbed, Joseph in the last brief moment before he descends into the valley of the shadow in which he will live for the rest of his life, Joseph whole, feeling fine before the Way of the Cross begins and no day will be without pain.

"I wanted to ask Sally a medical question," Joseph said, still unaware and unsuspecting. "My doctor just phoned me as I was leaving the office to tell me that my bilirubin count is up. I saw him yesterday because I noticed that my urine had turned brown. Sally asked if I had ever had hepatitis, but I haven't." He picked up his drink. "She made me promise that I would keep my next appointment with the doctor. I have to go to Minneapolis tomorrow, but I'll see him Thursday."

He seemed a notch more anxious as we finished our drinks and he prepared to leave. Overhearing just the muffled tone of his conversation with Sally had made me anxious. What's going on here, anyway?

We looked into each other's eyes as we waited in the foyer for the elevator. Its door opened and we gave each other an embrace. The door closed and I stood for a moment, my cup of foreboding overflowing, before I went back inside to read, uneasily and distractedly, until Sally arrived home, as filled with foreboding as I. Dear Joseph, what *was* going on? What did God want from you now? We slept poorly that night.

We did not see Joseph again until Saturday. On Thursday he had kept his appointment with his doctor, Warren Furey, a gentle man who seemed slightly bent, as if from so many years of listening carefully to his patients. Kenneth Velo, recently elected president of the Catholic Extension Society and now a monsignor, was with Joseph when Dr. Furey told him that the tests pointed to cancer of the pancreas and that, while the doctors were confident that they could remove the cancer, this illness would be what would end his life. Given the good shape he was in, and with the finest care available, Joseph stood a very good chance of being in that quarter of patients who live on for at least five years.

On Friday, Joseph had sat remarkably calm at the center of a storm of publicity that broke when, at a televised news conference, a team of doctors announced their findings and explained the Whipple method of surgery, which they intended to follow. He called us afterward, and Ken Velo, as shaken as we, confirmed later that "Eminence," as he affectionately called Joseph, wanted to see us on Saturday morning.

"How fragile it all is," Joseph said softly as we sat together in a parlor on the first floor of his residence. It was early Saturday afternoon, and Joseph had left the vicars of the archdiocese upstairs to visit for a while. He had called us at 6:44 that morning. He had to go to Loyola University Hospital for more blood work. Could he postpone our visit until early afternoon?

Sally looked up pancreatic cancer. "Insidious"—the textbook spoke harshly. "Six months." The disease causes no symptoms until it is so well established inside a person that nothing can be done about it.

And here sat Joseph, attacked again unfairly, Joseph who should be the pope, being called instead into a different mystery. I thought of—but only later quoted the words in a letter to Joseph—what Jesus prophesied to Peter: "When you are older you will stretch out your hands, and another will tie you fast and carry you off against your will." The words haunted me for months, for they identified Joseph's calling with Peter's. Yet I could not absorb it. It seemed so unfair— as guileful as this disease that had entered him like an evil spirit—that Joseph, who had just come through the worst of tests, should have crashed through the paper-veiled hoop of a cruel circus only to find death, sharp of claw and uncaged, waiting for him.

Visions of the mystery forced themselves on me as we three sat, as close together as bus passengers, our voices swallowed up by the rugs, drapes, and pillowed sofas of the residence. Joseph seemed so pale and vulnerable after having looked so well a few nights before. In the intervening time, he had completed the first of the traditional stations of the cross, for he had been judged, as Jesus was, in public and condemned to death. Of him, one might say, as Pilate did of the Lord, "Behold the man." For here was the quiet bravery that eluded the Hemingways of the world, the manliness in gentleness. Here, indeed, was a real man.

Try as I might, I could not wave away the outlines of the spiritual journey on which Joseph had now embarked. His calling had never been, in God's plan, to become the pope. He had been called to be within reach of the papacy and then to let go of it in a further working out of the spiritual dynamic with which he struggled every day. He had let go, and something greater was demanded of him.

He had been given a public life in which to live, again, in bored, postmodern times, the life of Jesus. Joseph, as he would demonstrate in the ensuing fourteen months, was a saint of the Roman Catholic Church or there were no saints at all. Joseph was a holy man in, of all places, Chicago.

"I wake in the night," he told us, "and I admit that I can feel fear without being afraid, that I can doubt without losing my faith. When I get out of the hospital, I am going to spend less time on administration and more time on pastoral work."

He seemed girded for the task as we embraced him and left him to rejoin his assistant bishops upstairs. "I'm getting everything arranged so there won't be any interruption. I'm delegating everything so the archdiocese will run just fine without me."

The next day, Sunday, Joseph spent hours in phone calls to sick priests before going, with Ken Velo, to the Cancer Center of Loyola University Hospital, just west of the city in Maywood. "I felt a shock," he told us later, "when I saw the sign that said CANCER in big letters, because it made me realize even more what was happening to me."

As he entered the hospital, waiting reporters asked him which was worse, the false accusation of sex abuse or the diagnosis of cancer. "The false accusation," he answered promptly, "was far worse. I can accept illness as part of the human condition, but a false accusation out of nowhere— that is harder to accept."

The next day, he underwent surgery that lasted well into the afternoon. The surgeons and Dr. Furey held a press conference later in the week, after all the test results were in, and while they imparted grave news about the reality of Joseph's cancer, they did so optimistically, confidently, predicting a return to work after his recovery and some vacation in Italy. We had a reprieve, I thought, only a reprieve, and there was no telling when it would be taken away from us.

Chapter 15

DEATH IS AT WORK IN ME,

BUT LIFE IN YOU.

— 2 CORINTHIANS 4:12

There are fourteen stations in the way of the Cross, and Joseph lived fourteen months from his initial cancer diagnosis to its recurrence, dying almost three years to the day after having been falsely accused of sexual abuse. There are no certainties in such matters, but knowing Joseph as I did, I knew that nothing ever injured him more than the charge that he had broken the trust that he placed first among the working virtues of his life as priest and bishop.

He was fond of the story that Sir Alec Guinness told in a memoir about playing Chesterton's Father Brown on location in France. At the end of a day's shooting, he started walking back to his hotel, still wearing the black soutane that was his costume for the part. A small boy greeted him, *Bon jour*, took his hand, and walked along with him until he reached his family home, where he bade the actor farewell, *Au revoir, mon père*. Guiness wrote of the overwhelming feeling of trust that the boy had placed in a man who was not a stranger because he was a priest. It was one of the motives for his own conversion to Catholicism.

That was the kind of trust people should expect from priests, Joseph thought; *that* is the kind of trust I want them to experience from me. That, indeed, was the kind of trust that everybody—whether a bishop or a bellboy—experienced in relationship, however brief, with Joseph. That explains why people—fellow bishops, parishoners, friends—felt so free in his presence: they were safe with him.

And so, in November 1993, that month of All Souls, dying light, and hints of killing frost, Joseph had been damaged throughout his being by the lies hurled at him. Those who targeted Joseph rationalized their attacks, as terrorists always do, as noble and necessary assaults on an enemy. The smug totalitarians who assailed Joseph never worried about whether they might harm or even kill an innocent person.

The cancer that led to Joseph's death in November 1996 invaded a man who by previous trials had already been raked and turned like garden earth into which the seeds of lies could be scattered by those who forged malign charges out of nothing, out of thin air, to plant in him. If, as in Thomistic philosophy, nothingness is the womb of evil, then those who played a role in savaging Joseph's character shared the midwifery of his death.

They were in it for varied motives, to be sure. Some, such as the questionably competent lawyer Rubino, may have dreamed less of righting a wrong than of filling their pockets.

Others, such as the Catholic zealots of the *Wanderer,* lacking the honor of genuine conservatives, kindled fires to burn imagined heretics. Let us inspect others, such as the pathetic Fiore, who hoped to garner esteem for himself to shore up a failed career. Let them stand together in the dock, for I accuse them of wanting nothing less than the destruction of Joseph Cardinal Bernardin and his work.

Chapter 16

THEY HAVE PIERCED MY HANDS AND FEET

AND NUMBERED ALL MY BONES.

— PSALM 22:16–17

Joseph came for a Christmastime meal, asking us, good mannered even in distress, if lunch would be okay.

Sure, what is good for you? We leave for Florida on the twenty-eighth.

Fine, Joseph answered in that mellow voice, as though he had no troubles. Wednesday, December 27, 1995.

He smiled broadly as he stepped out of the elevator, but as he slipped out of his overcoat he seemed as thin as the cane he was carrying. He was using the cane to balance his gaunt frame because he had now been diagnosed with spinal stenosis. As if his backbone were a hand, it was tightening its grip, winching excruciating pain out of the nerve tendrils in the vertebral column. Still, he was cheerful; it's not caused by the cancer. Doctor Gaynor, his oncologist, who was also a nun, told him that his regular tests showed that he was "cancer free."

How Joseph drew strength and confidence from that phrase, that mantra for his hope and determination, that light in his eye, that great-souled spirit. I'm beating this thing. So far, so good.

Joseph sipped the Manhattan he had requested from my wife. "Make it with your father's recipe, Sally," he had said, standing in the doorway of the kitchen, the same one he had passed through on that last evening of robust good health the previous June when he took the phone to ask Sally about the first signature symptoms of his illness.

He managed the drink in one hand and, in the other, the silver-headed black cane, whose subtle wink in the light matched Joseph's understated way, even of being ill. We chatted before a lunch of filet mignon. I have since prayed that his, at this last of our holiday feasts, was not as tough as mine. How human, Sally and I have also thought, that a great grief can be kindled by so small a memory. Yet Joseph seemed to enjoy his lunch and to talk without complaint about this new problem.

He shifted often for a better position on his chair. I could not banish the thought that Joseph had taken his first steps on the *via dolorosa,* the way of sorrow. We stood at that station in the *via crucis* at which they lower the cross onto Jesus' back. Here, now, in this darkening December, the same rude cross had been laid on Joseph's.

He spoke of the new ministry that had arisen around his weekly visits for treatment at the Loyola Cancer Center. There, the other cancer patients spontaneously sought him out—please pray for me, my mother, my husband, my cousin. The prayer list finally exceeded six hundred, and Joseph spent a good deal of time answering letters from cancer patients, calling them on the phone or visiting them, particularly the children, in the hospital. "I've never felt more like a priest," he said, as if this work were a great gift to him rather than to those to whom he ministered so naturally.

People stopped by his residence to leave prayer requests; others asked if they could bring the sick to him for his blessing. At public events, people approached him just to touch him, or touch a newborn babe to his arm. "I thought they were just trying to get my attention at first," Joseph said, still puzzled at such interest in him. Yet this was what people have spontaneously done throughout history with those they understand to be holy.

"The doctors tell me," Joseph said, changing the subject, "that they might be able to relieve this stenosis with surgery."

"Have you," Sally asked, "considered getting a second opinion"—Joseph cocked his head, his brown eyes large behind his outsize glasses—"from somebody like Len Cerullo, for instance?" She meant Dr. Leonard Cerullo of Columbus Hospital, one of the most distinguished neurosurgeons in Chicago.

"Oh, I know Len. He doesn't think I should have the surgery." It was clear from Joseph's tone that he preferred the choice of surgery, some action and soon, that had a chance of lessening the acute pain in his back. "Len takes a more conservative approach."

The conversation took another turn as Joseph spoke of the Christmas services and liturgies in which he had participated during the past few days. He seemed to be savoring them—or was that my imagination again, sensing hints of last times and last chances in everything?

Joseph thanked us for the flowers we had sent him. We had begun to send them every Saturday, and Ken Velo had told us how eagerly Eminence anticipated their arrival. In a classic example of how indirectly and gently Joseph could address a potentially delicate issue, he had pointed one day when I was in his rooms that season to the week's flowers at the side of his desk. Look at these.

Subtle they were not, this squashed mass of unidentifiable red and white blooms, and surely not the "delicate and tasteful" ones we had ordered. We changed florists the next week and Joseph had a good laugh when I told him about it. The flowers, as he later informed me, improved right away.

Joseph rose slowly to leave. "They feel better," he said with a big smile, "when I'm in my office." "They" were his staff. We helped him into his coat and saw him down to his car, a silver Buick Park Avenue that he was still driving for himself. We embraced and wished one another a happy new year. He expected a good one, with improved health and less pain, but we feared that it might not be so as he waved and then drove off into the stream of Lake Shore Drive traffic leading downtown.

It was Sunday, January 28, 1996, and we were in Florida. I had completed the first essay in the text for a book, *This Man Bernardin*, that featured the photographs that John White, Pulitzer Prize–winning photographer of the *Chicago Sun-Times,* had taken of Joseph even before he became Chicago's archbishop. John's artist's eye had seen Joseph's kindness and genuineness in their first casual meeting, when Joseph had come to Chicago for some event at the end of the seventies. "I remember," John said, "when he stopped to talk to me, he wasn't just being nice. I could feel his concern all through me."

I had faxed a copy of my essay to Joseph, who seemed very pleased with it. We retired at about 10 P.M. I awakened, jolted out of the deep well of dreams, at eleven-thirty and had a hard time getting back to sleep. Early the following morning I flew to New York for meetings of our family business. When I got back to my hotel room after a dinner meeting, there was a voice mail message from Sally: "Joe called. He said to tell you, 'Something has happened.' He wants you to call."

Joseph answered his private phone. Ken Velo had placed it, for convenience, in his bed. "Last night," he explained in a voice worn as brass fittings are by time and wear, "I was climbing the stairs. It was ten-thirty or so. I fell, and nobody could hear me. I had to crawl inch by inch to my room. The pain was excruciating. I finally got to a phone and they came to help me. The doctor says I have another fracture in my spine. The radiation is weakening my bones, so when something like that happens, they just snap."

We talked for several minutes. That was all he wanted to do, say freely what he felt to an old friend in a passageway that was narrowing and growing dimmer. I hung up the phone and sat on the edge of my bed. Ten-thirty last night. That was eleven-thirty in Florida. That's when I was startled awake.

I did not sleep much and rose before first light to write Joseph a letter to send to him by Federal Express. Long before, I had made a policy of not making copies of letters that I wanted to belong only to those who received them. Old Irish superstition? Hard to say, but it enabled me to write from the heart without thinking about it.

I can only recall the general feeling that possessed me as I wrote. Joseph, like Jesus on the *via crucis,* had fallen the first time. Joseph had been called, at the time I thought he would be pope, to live out a Passion Play of Gospel values, of faith and suffering that was redeeming the rest of us. Joseph was dying for our sins. And what could I do, except accompany him as closely as possible and perhaps, as Veronica does, at another Station of the Cross, hold up a cloth to cleanse his face, to bring this smallest of comforts to dear Joseph, the shape of whose journey was now clear to me? According to tradition, she had taken away an image of Jesus on the cloth. Joseph wasn't going to get any better. He had begun his journey to Golgotha. I could make Joseph laugh a little, telling him that, in an old Catholic tradition, I was offering up for him the meetings I had to attend at our family business.

I also knew, however, that Joseph, confined now to his quarters, was doing everything he could to get well, to cast off this armored suit of illness that had been fitted to him so suddenly and return to his full schedule. He wanted people to see him as winning, not losing, this struggle. He had been that way the previous October when Sally and I had met him and Ken Velo in Rome. Joseph had been so proud to say that he had run a meeting of Roman officials that day and it had gone well. "They could all see," he said with a big smile, "that I'm functioning very well."

When I next talked to him, he thanked me simply, as was

his way, in a few words, as if my letter had been an expected response, one he could count on, as we both counted on each other.

The trouble was, of course, that, for the moment, Joseph was confined most of the time to his bed while the fracture healed. Rumors about his condition had swept through Chicago. The next Saturday, February 3, reporter Mary Ann Ahern called me in Florida. Was there any truth to the story that the cardinal was dying, that his health had deteriorated badly, that it was just a question of time?

I phoned Joseph immediately. "Have her call me after we hang up," he responded. "It's better to nip this in the bud right away." He called me back later to say that he had invited Mary Ann and her film crew to come to the residence for an interview for the evening news. She got an exclusive, and Joseph squelched a rumor. Perhaps Mary Ann, rather than I, had the role of Veronica. I could not help but think that, for all the love Chicago had for Joseph, there was an impersonal Chicago as well, watching Joseph as the throngs had watched Jesus as he made his way to Calvary.

So it went on for months as we kept in almost daily contact with Joseph, exchanging phone and fax messages. I finished the essays to accompany John White's photographs and wrote, at Joseph's request, the preface to that book. It came close enough to what he wanted to say that he signed it as his own. There was comfort still in working together in this quiet way.

We were back in Chicago when Joseph celebrated his sixty-eighth birthday, on April 2, 1996. "I'm not old yet," Joseph said to me on the phone, "but I seem to be heading in that direction." He was still able to smile even as he confided, "Yesterday I reached for a folder on my desk and I heard a bone snap. This osteoporis they say I now have is aggravated by the radiation. So I'm beginning consultations about possible surgery, to get some relief, I hope."

Joseph's negotiations and examinations continued over the next several weeks. He presided at a reception in his residence on a misty cool evening, June 16, 1996, anticipating for the American Booksellers Convention the formal publication date of John White's picture book, *This Man Bernardin*. It was remarkable, Sally and I thought as Joseph leaned heavily on his cane to hear some advice from Eppie Lederer, the famous columnist known as Ann Landers, that he could enjoy this attention so much. It flowed over him like a waterfall and he was not drowned but rather cleansed by it. In a way, Joseph loved the attention. He could even comment on it with a distanced smile, as if he had long ago sorted out what was lasting in life and what was not. Letting go of celebrations such as this, I could see, gave him great freedom.

He autographed a copy of the book, recapitulating the links of our lives, "To Gene and Sally with thanks for sticking with me during so many ups and downs over so many years . . . Joe." It is a treasured possession, but I could not help feeling then that it was a summing up, a bittersweet message that, as when I left the priesthood, we had reached a fork in the road and that he knew that he would soon be going on ahead.

Joseph left for Italy a week or so later with Father Scott Donahue as his companion for what was, as he told me after he returned, the most enjoyable trip he had ever made, to

visit his many cousins in the town, tucked into the top of Italy's boot, from which his parents came. "We talked after the meals," Joseph said, "on and on. That's about all we did, but it was wonderful."

There was a finished quality in Joseph's way of speaking about this pilgrimage to a place both sacred and comforting for him. When he returned he began serious explorations regarding surgery on his back. He had accepted an invitation from Dr. Cerullo to come out to his suburban home for dinner on Friday, August 2. Cerullo had suggested that Joseph would do better with some less invasive treatments for his back problems. But Joseph, after helicoptering to Madison, Wisconsin, courtesy of a friend, to consult with a specialist from the university there, had all but decided on what he would do. The surgery was set for September 16. Cerullo was not surprised by this decision. Joseph, he felt, did not want to hear his dissenting opinion. Surgery seemed to promise relief much more quickly than Cerullo's treatment plan.

Indeed, Joseph had told me of the pleasant dinner the next morning on the phone. "Len is full of it," Joseph said with a little flash of feeling, just such a spark as a man might strike when he is afraid that the other man is right after all. But Joseph loved the Cerullos even if he did not like Len's advice. Len was intimating what Joseph was not yet ready to accept— that he was not really well enough for surgery. On the way out, Joseph had admired a rosemary bush and brought home the cutting Len made and gave it to Sister Lucia, the bright and devoted nun who kept the residence running.

* * *

Back in April of 1996, I had developed what I termed "writer's leg" by working with my right leg wrapped around the steel leg of my chair without moving for several hours. The subsequent pain was later diagnosed as the evil flower of an injury to the peroneal nerve of my leg, similar to those suffered by people with their legs in stirrups in operating or delivery rooms. The course of medication resembled a bell curve, spread over several weeks.

I had just completed the tapering-off phase by the third week of August. Joseph suggested to me that it was a sign of age, chuckling that I would catch up with him in years on my birthday, Wednesday, August 28, 1996.

On the afternoon of that day, Sally and I worked in the gardens at our home in Michigan. The weather cast a clear blue eye on us. The Democrats were having a perfect week for their Chicago convention. At about three in the afternoon, the leg I thought was cured suddenly erupted in pain, as if someone had jabbed me with a knife. I retreated to the house, where rest eased the pain, and made it out to dinner with our neighbors.

When we returned, there was a message on our answering machine. "Hello. Gene, this is Joe. It is very important that I speak with you this evening." There was then a slight pause before—in a tone long familiar to me, one of longing, of holding on rather than letting go, one of rue for all that goes unnamed or undone in anybody's life—"Thank you, Gene."

Joseph answered the phone. "Gene," he said calmly, directly, the shock buffed half away, "Dr. Gaynor tells me that my cancer has returned. This afternoon she discovered five nodules on the liver. We may try a new drug that could be of some use. She tells me that I have a year to live, that I've got plenty of good days ahead yet."

We'll be in first thing tomorrow, I said.

Fine, he responded. I'd like you to help me write the statement I'll give on Friday.

Chapter 17

Sally dropped me at the residence, different now in the late-August sun, solemn and silent as a monk huddled in prayer. Sister Lucia let me in and we embraced, the only language in which the many people who loved Joseph could speak to one another. Ken Velo came down the stairs and we hugged each other, too. "He's waiting for you," Ken whispered gently. We shared an unspoken feeling of tenderness about Joseph, a feeling that our friend upstairs was not a powerful cardinal archbishop but rather an innocent boy, the best boy you would ever know, kept out of the sunlight now by a cowardly illness.

Joseph stood waiting at the top of the stairs. We held each other for a wordless moment. Was I imagining that he was also embracing God's will, that he wanted to let go of everything if that is what the Lord wanted, and that all that meaning lay gently in his greeting? We walked into his study, crammed with books, citations, and plaques. Above us in the dusky light of one lamp hung the painting he owned when I first met him, *Blue Desk,* as Joseph called it, for it was no more than that, this Wyethlike study of a desk lying in a field, a picture that in all its wistfulness, its summons of the deeper mysteries of every day, spoke to Joseph and of him at the same time.

He was not self-pitying, nor was he a stoic. He felt the weight of his illness, this enemy within, wily and watchful, that, like a thief who knew when you were off guard, had come out of hiding—for he had never really gone; Joseph never was "cancer free." That, as I came soon to learn, was one of the hardest parts of this *via crucis.* The betraying illness was the Judas of this Passion Play.

Joseph spoke positively, not falsely, of the year of grace he had left. He would immediately begin to seek a coadjutor bishop to come to Chicago so that he could prepare him to take on the running of the archdiocese, a job, aside from its central spiritual dimension, at least as demanding as being the CEO of General Motors. "I want to try to get the right man." Joseph paused and smiled, not prompted by humor but by wisdom, by what he knew about the Church and his brother bishops. "The pickings," he said, "are pretty slim."

Joseph talked briefly of old times, of Archbishop Hallinan and Cardinal Dearden, the great leaders and mentors who had also been stricken with illnesses that ended their careers early. Then he turned to the present again. "I'm not surprised that Jim and Bernie have criticized the Common Ground proposal." He was referring to his most recent initiative, an effort to draw together Catholics from the conservative and liberal sides in order to discover what they really believed in together and to enable them to talk together to reduce friction and criticism within the body of the Church.

Bernie was Bernard Cardinal Law, central casting's handsome white-haired, red-cheeked archbishop of Boston. Jim was James Cardinal Hickey, the gentle archbishop of Washington, D.C. Each in a different but equally cutting way had attacked Joseph's proposal as unnecessary: we already have Common Ground, the teachings of the Catholic Church.

Joseph shook his head sadly. Their remarks had cut deeply, not only because they had been made so quickly but because they had broken the protocol that cardinals never took issue with one another in public. "That's Mother Hickey for you," I said, using an affectionate nickname that other bishops used for Jim because of his cautious ways and sweet disposition.

Joseph smiled. "*Grand*mother Hickey," he said with a laugh, as close as Joseph ever came to saying a harsh word about somebody else. "If another pope came in, who is more flexible than John Paul II, they would support this right away."

He rose and we walked toward his office, a few steps beyond the study that lay, book-filled but windowless, at the quiet center of his suite of rooms. "I've got a lot of preparation to do for my death. I'm not going to leave Ken Velo and everybody in the lurch, wondering what to do." He sat down at his desk, looked up at me expectantly.

"I'll tell you what, Joe," I said. "I'll leave the room and you write what comes to you. You call me when you're ready, and then we can go over it together."

He nodded, unscrewed his pen, began to write on a yellow legal-size pad, straight lines in blue ink. I walked out of the room and sat in a parlor. The quiet in the house seemed like a force of nature, a weight on the spirit we would all have to shrug off if we were to stand with Joseph in any helpful way. It was still hard to think of Joseph as ill, or the residence as soundless, so much life and light had he brought into it.

He called me and I came into his office and sat down. He read the words he would deliver at a press conference at the archdiocesan offices the next afternoon. "Is that okay?" he asked, the quintessential Bernardin inquiry. Does it need something here, or more there? What do you think?

"Don't change a word of it," I said, echoing his words to me twenty years before about what I had written on the same kind of paper about why I wanted to get married. He smiled, squared the pages off. One big job done. "I've got to call Cacciavillan now," he said, referring to the papal pro-nuncio in Washington, D.C., who would inform the pope of the recurrence of Joseph's illness.

The press conference the next day was held in a cramped room. Joseph seemed serene, as he had been just before when Sally, Ken Velo, and the auxiliary bishops and other staff members, had gathered in his office. Joseph read his statement in a lilting voice, its Southern lining warming each word, a tone inspirited by his belief, as he told the reporters, that death "is a friend."

Death was no friend to the young reporters jostling for better positions in front of him. They carried gym bags and water bottles, didn't smoke, and dreamed of living, young and lithe, forever. Joseph loved them nonetheless and had mentioned the unmentionable—death—on this sunny last Friday of August. Joseph had brought it up and suddenly everybody in the room felt that they, too, might admit mortality into their thoughts.

"We can look on death as an enemy," Joseph said, "or we can look on it as a friend. If we see it as an enemy, death causes anxiety and fear. We need to go into a state of denial. But if we see it as a friend, our attitude is truly different. As a person of faith, I see death as a friend, as the transition from earthly life to the eternal."

He would keep a full schedule and keep everyone informed. He spoke of the Catholic people of Chicago, whom he treasured, and saved some last graceful words for the media spread before him. "We have enjoyed a good professional relationship in the years I have been archbishop of Chicago—and this will continue. Now I ask that you stand with me personally. Whatever your religious affiliation may be, I ask that you say a prayer for me. And in return I will pray for you and your loved ones." He concluded by reading one of his favorite prayers, that of Saint Francis. How filled with peace his voice sounded as he intoned, "Lord, make me an instrument of your peace . . . "

Joseph nodded as the questions began. Why are you telling us this now? "Because," Joseph said, "you are part of my family." Then, with a perfectly timed shrug and a smile, "And if I didn't, you'd find out anyway."

The reporters laughed and then, as Joseph turned away, began to applaud, the only tribute available to them, the only way that they could say, We love you, too.

Sally went back and sat with Joseph in his office while I stayed behind, providing some kind of rough cover by answering questions, some silly (did the cardinal wait until today so as not to interrupt the Democratic convention?), some more searching (how can the cardinal face something like this so calmly?).

We slept uneasily that night, for Joseph lived in both our dreams. In mine, he said, I'm going to write a little book before I die but I'd like to read it to you as I go along.

In Sally's dream, however, Joseph and she were sitting in his office as he said to her, You know, Sally, I'm only going to live until November.

Both dreams came true. Joseph had known the truth about himself at a deep level and had communicated it to the deepest levels of our beings on that last Friday of the last August of his life.

Chapter 18

The last enemy that

shall be destroyed

is death.

— 1 Corinthians 15:26

It was late on Labor Day afternoon in 1996, the end of summer, the scene of transition all across the country. I called to see how Joseph was doing.

"Okay," he said, not hiding the wistfulness. "I've spent some time throwing things out. And I called Steven Cook's mother. I had heard from some priests in Cincinnati that people were blaming Steven for my illness, that it even got into the papers. So I wanted her to know that I didn't feel that way, that I thought Steven was a fine young man who had been wronged by others. I wanted to reassure her, but the poor woman has been through so much, I'm not sure that I could."

On a rainy day in late September, Joseph flew to Rome with Monsignor Kenneth Velo. Joseph asked the members of the media not to follow him on this journey, and they respected his wishes. Joseph and Ken would see the pope and visit the Vatican office that appointed bishops. Joseph was thinking about his beloved Chicago. He did not want it to be without a good shepherd for very long after his death.

On that same day, the damaged nerve in my right leg flared up, as the doctors had said that it might, and for the whole time Joseph was away, I was in extraordinary pain. Was I paying the price for my sins, or was this a small opportunity to share in and perhaps relieve the sufferings that were constant for my brother Joseph? As I was taken by wheelchair from one hospital department to another, I thought of Joseph and of how clearly he was living again for us the life of Jesus in the unlikely setting of Chicago.

I thought, too, of September 17, 1996, when, along with Ken Velo and another close friend, Kevin Dowdle, Joseph and I had driven through veils of late-summer heat to the penitentiary at Joliet, about an hour southwest of Chicago. A murderer scheduled for execution that night had asked Joseph to visit him. Joseph, his back propped by a pillow, was hunched with me in the backseat. He opened the prayer book he had brought with him and pointed to a line: "I was in prison and you visited me." He nodded. "That's why I'm making this trip."

The warden met us on the highway and led us on a bumpy, unpaved back road through a gate great enough to have opened on Jerusalem. The prison, where Leopold and Loeb had been jailed for the thrill murder of Bobby Franks in the Twenties, was in lockdown, as it had been for many months. Our eyes roved the cement buildings, some the color of cof-

fee and some the color of sand, the central one fashioned like a great wheel, another shaped like a silo, and yet another like a hulking Foreign Legion fort. A piece of paper scuffed along in a dust devil whirling across the utterly silent yard.

Joseph climbed out of the car and started walking toward a low brick building in which the only prisoner was the man who was to die at midnight. Joseph had written letters to the families of the man's victims that morning. As he was halfway across the old hard dirt path, scored with rivulets dug by a thousand rainstorms, voices began shouting from the slitted windows cut into the bare blank walls of the prison buildings.

"Hey, Bernardin," one slashed down like a saber swipe, "you fucking priest!"

A passage from station to station through the crowd to speak to the man on death row now, who, like the good thief already on his cross, might yet ask for mercy on the day he was to die.

"Hey, Bernardin . . ." The catcalls rained down invisibly and were suddenly shut out as we entered the building, dismal with broken tiles and toilet, all its windows blacked out, as was the custom on the day of an execution.

Joseph walked with the warden to the hallway at the end of the corridor. Above it hung a placard, printed by hand on the back of a shirt cardboard: "This Is Not an Exit." It might as well have read, "Abandon Hope," for this was the stub end of death row. The door closed behind Joseph, and although we could watch him through the wire-meshed glass door, we could not hear him.

I can never forget the scene. Joseph, dying soon, his ringed right hand holding the left hand, thrust through the bars, of the prisoner dying that night. The condemned man's dreadlocks moved as he leaned toward Joseph to tell him something or to hear him read from the scriptures. Joseph, listening patiently, as he had so often to the sad stories of so many people, never shocked, always ready to understand and forgive a sinner. Joseph would forgive us all, he was indeed dying for our sins. Jesus and the penitent thief in a place as desperate as Golgotha itself.

As Jesus had encountered his mother on the way to Golgotha, so Joseph visited his mother regularly in a nursing home, where she was cared for by the Little Sisters of the Poor. His last visit would be just a few weeks before his death. She would be ninety-two in November, and although she recognized him, this was usually in flashes of consciousness, pokes into time from which she would retreat quickly. Still, the power of this living out again of Jesus' farewell to his mother was very great.

Joseph would also be denounced by the high priests, for their equivalent was found among his brother bishops who were anxious to criticize him for his advocacy of the Common Ground project. Only Roger Cardinal Mahoney of Los Angeles stood by him to the end.

For Joseph was on his way to what would be, in many ways, a public death, and although the heavens would not erupt, they would lay the first mantle of snow on his tomb on the fast-falling night of his burial. Joseph bore the weight of these good-byes.

What do you do, Joseph? his mother sometimes still asked.

I work for the Church, Mother.

They don't pay very well, do they?

The mixture of good humor and sadness was heartwrenching, this eternal story of separation and death lived out before our eyes. Wherever there is time, as Joseph Campbell put it, there is sorrow. And we were in the midst of that mystery with Joseph, with the sands drifting lower each day even as our sense of being with a holy man grew deeper.

How proud his mother would have been at the White House on September 9, the day after a major storm had scoured the grit off the city of Washington and left its buildings sparkling clean. The East Room, crowded with dignitaries, guests, and reporters, was bathed by gentle light. Joseph, pale and spare as the waning moon, bowed as President Clinton placed the Presidential Medal of Freedom on his shoulders. He smiled later midst the bustling reception in the Red Room. Yes, he had noticed that he received the greatest round of applause of any of the distinguished honorees. "Not bad," he said softly, "for a little boy from Columbia, South Carolina." In the reception line, Hillary Clinton spoke glowingly of Cardinal Bernardin.

He is luminous, I observed. "Yes, yes," she said enthusiastically. *"Luminous,* that's the word. *He is luminous."*

Chapter 19

NONE OF US LIVES AS HIS OWN MASTER AND NONE OF US DIES AS HIS OWN MASTER. WHILE WE LIVE, WE ARE RESPONSIBLE TO THE LORD, AND WHEN WE DIE, WE DIE AS HIS SERVANTS.

— ROMANS 14:7

It was late in the evening on a Sunday in October. We were sitting in Joseph's study, each of us with a cane now. We had just climbed the stairs together, a pair of wounded veterans, I said to Joseph. Yes, we have been through many battles at that.

I had placed my cane on the floor in front of his coffee table. I was sitting at the end of the couch. Joseph's worn prayer book lay just below the glass bell holding the Laetare Medal he had received from Notre Dame the year before. The old house held us just as silently.

Joseph, at the other end of the couch, put his hand to his forehead, spoke quietly, reflectively. He had been working on his book, *The Gift of Peace,* sending chapters as he finished them to Father Al Spilly to edit and put into his computer. "You know," he said softly, as if he did not have to search for this conviction, so present was it in his being, "I'm grateful that I am beyond posturing now." He sighed. "I feel sorry for many of my friends who are still caught up in it."

He turned directly toward me. "When Ken and I were in Rome, I visited the proper congregation to see about getting a coadjutor bishop appointed here in Chicago. The head of the congregation was not in, so I spoke to a deputy. He seemed amazed that I would do such a thing. 'What are you doing this for,' he asked me, 'giving up your authority? I'd never do it. Why do you want to do it?' " He turned his gaze away from me, shook his head.

The phone at his side rang. It was Cardinal Law from Boston, asking how he was. Fine, Bernie. Yes, that worked out fine, and thanks so much. "You know," he said to me, "you're the only one of my friends who understands how much just talking on the phone takes out of me. My other friends, who out of the goodness of their hearts are calling, are killing me, asking how I am."

Joseph picked up a folder from the coffee table, handed it to me. "These are the notes I made at a retreat with Bishop Bob Morneau of Green Bay a few years ago. I want you to have this copy. I Xeroxed it myself. Would you mind reading them with me?"

I looked down at the lined pages filled with Joseph's fine handwriting, fine as that of the surgeon he might have been, laying his soul open here, in this half-light, all the light that was left for him.

Joseph had marked the first entry with scriptural references: REV. 3: 20—GIVING UP and LUKE 1—ANNUNCIATION—TRUST. These were the themes of his life, the chant sounding in his soul as it did in medieval churches, the yearnings of his spirit as he faced death. My mouth was dry as I began to read.

I want desperately to open the door to let the Lord in so he can take over my soul completely. Yet I seem unable to do so. I let him come in partway. I talk with him but I am afraid to let him take over. Why?

I want to succeed. I want to be acknowledged as one who succeeds. I am very upset when I read or hear criticisms about my decisions/actions. This drive causes me to want to *control* things, make them come out "right." For this reason, I tend not to put full confidence in people until they have proved their competence.

My voice cracked slightly as I continued.

I deal with the Lord in the same way. Conceptually, I know he can and should be trusted. It is his church; nothing happens that is beyond his purview. Yet I seem to be unwilling to let go. Is it because, at times, I fear that his will may be different from mine, and that if his will wins out I will be criticized? Is it because, psychologically and emotionally, I have simply not been able to let go?

I paused, for here was the struggle Joseph had described many times, that longing to let go, that desire to trust wholly in God that had been the theme of these weeks and months since that last night when he looked across the lake at the lighted Ferris wheel and said that he would go with me if I would take a ride on it.

Is part of the cause of this the fact that so many people each day make demands on me? Is it because their expectations are so numerous, direct, and personal that I cannot free myself from their pressure? Is there a certain pride that causes me not to risk letting go? Am I paralyzed to some extent by the fact that at times I am caught between the more progressive elements of the Church, who expect me to carry their banner, and the more conservative elements (including my peers and the Holy See), who expect me to support their agenda? Sometimes this tension causes me not to state what I *really* think.

Joseph took up the reading in soft, Southern tones.

Do I refuse to let the Lord come in all the way because I am afraid he will insist on certain things (in terms of my personal life) that I am reluctant or unwilling to do or give up?

Twelve years ago, I gave away all the money I had and said I would never again have a savings account or stocks, that I would keep only what was needed to maintain my checking account. Even though I deposit almost all my honoraria in a special account of the archdiocese which is for various purposes, even though I give away a substantial portion of my personal funds each year, in the last year or two I have been given so many gifts that I now have a savings account again on the pretext that I may need it for Mother, or myself later on. I need to take a look at this again.

I interrupted. "Joe, you should be as understanding of yourself as you have always been of the rest of us. You cannot be hard on yourself when you are gentle with us sinners."

He nodded, his glasses glinting in the low light that hid his eyes from me. Letting go—that was what he really wanted to do as fully and finally as he could, as he would read from a later page about what would be required for him to be what the Lord expected him to be.

To do the above—and more—requires that I truly *love* the Lord, more than anything/one else—*trust* him, really trust him as he accompanies me on his journey— "let myself go," which can only be done if there is a lot of *love* and *trust*.

Joseph paused, looked up at me, read again.

It is the "letting myself go" that is related to Jesus' "emptying himself."

Joseph turned to a later page of his notes, where he had reflected on Saint Paul's relationship to the Philippians, which, in its demands, complications, and opportunities, seemed to match his own with his people.

He read a quotation from chapter three of Paul to the Philippians.

> I wish to know Christ, and the *power in him* . . . "I wish to know Christ and the *power* flowing from his resurrection; likewise to know *how to share in his sufferings.* . . . Thus do I hope that I may arrive at the resurrection from the dead."

But Joseph, I thought then even as I do now, you have reached this point, you have emptied yourself, you do know Christ and make us feel his power through you. You are sharing in his sufferings.

He read me his soul-searching resolutions, the summation of his spiritual goals, which, with death but a few weeks off, he was still striving for as mightily as Saint Paul. Joseph had drawn me close, I knew, but, giving me these retreat notes as he did, he was really letting go. The time was short and he had to let go of everything if he was to be fit for the journey ahead. When we finished and embraced, he bent down and retrieved my cane. "I can do that better than you," he said good-humoredly. He saw me down the steps and out into the night.

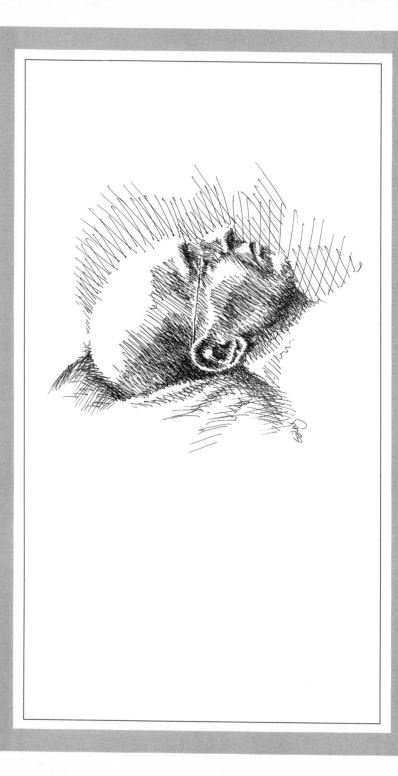

Chapter 20

THIS ONE THING I DO, FORGETTING THOSE

THINGS THAT ARE BEHIND, AND

REACHING FORTH INTO THOSE

THINGS WHICH ARE BEFORE.

I PRESS TOWARD THE MARK.

— PHILIPPIANS 3:13–14

It was Ken Velo, calling from the residence. "Come over," he said gently, "and lay your hand in blessing on your great friend's forehead." It was a cold November night and I had known that Joseph's final letting go was near. We had stayed away from the residence. Joseph had given up day-to-day operations of the archdiocese in mid-October and, after a heroic effort to be present at the renaming of the Loyola Cancer Center after him on October 29, had not left the residence again. Many people who should be there, such as his nephews and nieces, had come, and many who knew Joseph far less well than we did pressed for a last visit with him.

He had asked Sally and me to come for afternoon Mass on November 8 but by midday was so overcome with fatigue that he had to call it off. We sent him the regular Saturday flowers, and Ken kept them from being lost in the other baskets that had begun to arrive. Hundreds of ordinary citizens had begun placing flowers and candles on the entrance steps on North State Parkway.

Knowing he did not need an extra phone call, I wrote Joseph a fax every day instead. When he responded, his penmanship had come loose as a sail might from a mast and had begun to flutter slightly on the page. He was desperately trying to finish his book, and Jeremy Langford, the bright young editor from Loyola Press, was trying to compile the last of it for him. The completed manuscript of *The Gift of Peace,* which would become a best-seller after his death, was placed in his lap by Ken Velo on the last morning of his life.

It was not easy to stay away, yet it seemed to be our role in the great mystery of letting go that Joseph had entered. We had to let him go, we had to let him be about his Father's business. Still, as we climbed the stairs to his room, past the guarding policeman, past his dear sister, Elaine, and his oncologist, Dr. Gaynor, a hundred other visions of ascending these stairs flashed in my mind.

Joseph was sitting in a chair next to his bed, wearing a dark shirt and black pants. Lying in bed was too painful for his back. He breathed deeply, gasped. He could not keep his head up. Sister Lucia came in, adjusted a straw in the glass of 7-Up she held just below his face. "The doctor," she whispered, "said that you should take some of this." He drew on the straw, obedient, I thought, obedient unto death.

Sister Lucia took away the glass, glanced sadly at us before leaving the room and closing the door. Sally and I were alone with Joseph, the house, the city shut out. The past was mingled with and was inseparable from this moment.

Joseph twisted in his chair uncomfortably. Sally bent down, rearranged his position, trying to make him more comfortable. He raised his head as a man does warding off the deepest of sleeps, looked into Sally's face, a few inches now from his own. "Oh, Sally!" he sighed, and his head dropped back onto his chest. An embrace and a letting go.

Tears glistened in Sally's eyes as she straightened up. "I'm going to see if I can get something to make Joe more comfortable," she said and slipped out of the room. Joseph coughed, raised his head toward me, caught my eyes for a moment, tried to say something. If I could not understand the word, I had not missed his eyes, those eyes I had first looked into across a meeting table a generation and a half before. Yes, we understood each other, we could count on each other for the long haul.

Joseph sighed. His head bobbed. He could not raise it again. Mucus began to flow from his nose, to spread on his lips. I stood up, reached in my pocket for a clean handkerchief, and as tenderly as I could, wiped his face. As I pulled the damp linen back, I was so struck by my realization that my hand trembled: this was a Station of the Cross and I had indeed been granted Veronica's role of cleansing the face of Christ.

I stood over my old friend, placed my hands on his head. "Dear Joe," I whispered, "we all love you." Then I blessed him with the Latin formula I had not forgotten: *"Benedictio Dei Omnipotentis, Patris et Filii et Spiritus Sancti, descendat super te et maneat semper."* I leaned down, half embraced him, and kissed him on the forehead.

Sally returned with Sister Lucia and they fixed some pillows to relieve Joseph a little. He was breathing more heavily now and his head was on his chest. We stood up. Sally touched his head. "We love you, Joe," she said. We walked out of the room.

Joseph Cardinal Bernardin—our dear brother Joseph—died at 1:30 A.M. the next morning, November 14, 1996.

Chapter 21

"'PEACE' IS MY FAREWELL TO YOU,

MY PEACE IS MY GIFT TO YOU."

— JOHN 14:25–31

The great ceremony of Joseph's funeral was an extraordinary outpouring of grief and gratitude, grief at his death and gratitude for his life. At the very center of the funeral, Ken Velo concluded his remarkable sermon as he had ended so many trips with Joseph. "Cardinal. Eminence. You're home. You're home." These words, which made us feel that we were seeing Joseph into paradise, set sadness to flight and freed our joyful sense that Joseph was with God in eternity. Only a hundred cars were allowed in the cortege that followed Joseph's body to the Bishops' Tomb, west of the city, but thousands upon thousands lined the eighteen miles of streets, holding candles against the falling night. The sun had just set as we arrived at the cemetery. As we sang "Amazing Grace" in the dark that spread down and away from the lighted tomb, a fine

snow began to fall. Iron-filing snowflakes danced in the head-lights of the departing cars. Our cardinal, our Eminence, our brother Joseph was home at last.

We let go, we thought, but Joseph has not left us. He is with us, our brother Joseph, *my* friend Joseph, but if he gives us comfort, he is not likely to give us rest. For Joseph loved the best in all things. He will not allow us to go forth with clear consciences if, remembering him and the Lord he preached, we do less than we are capable of in anything we do. I have complained that he is trying to reform my life before I am ready for it. Many of us claim small miracles, grace notes in our lives that others might not notice and many would not even acknowledge.

But they are special, as though designed for each of us in-dividually, and almost all of them ask something more of us, as he incessantly demanded more of himself. Joseph is just warming up with these remembrances, I tell people, just get-ting the hang of being the saint we recognized him to be.

So let one small miracle stand for them all. On the morn-ing that Joseph died, Dr. Cerullo's wife called to him, Come here, Len, look at this rosemary plant, the one the cardinal took a cutting from last August. The plant had never bloomed before and it has not bloomed since. But here, on a morning when clouds of breath trailed us all, on this bitter dawn of No-vember 14, a single purple bloom had emerged.

"There's rosemary," Shakespeare writes, "that's for re-membrance."

I must always keep my eyes focused on Jesus. He must be the center of my life. I must "let go" so he can work in and through me. I must visualize the Jesus with whom I am intimately united, with whom I am in love (I must not be afraid to say this) as a real friend, a manly person who — even though he is God's Son — shares all the human feelings & experience: joy, sorrow, doubt, anxiety, etc.; one who will give me strength and support; one who understands and loves me despite my sins and weaknesses; one who will embrace me and give me comfort and a sense of security if I let him. In short, I must TRUST him completely. If I do I have nothing to fear — regardless of the pain and frustration of the present moment.

From the personal journals of Joseph Cardinal Bernardin